REVIEWS

How many of us want to grow up to be like our mothers? If women's groups are any indication, virtually none. The anguish that surfaces when women speak about their ambivalence toward their mothers is heart-rendering. But a woman who wants to do something about this has a real dilemma. As one woman put it, "If I find anything good in my mother, I don't want to be like her, so I can't have that. But if I don't find anything good in her, then who am I?"

Fortunately for us, Marilyn Boynton and Mary Dell have drawn on their extensive research and experience to give us some direction in this complicated territory. Sandra Butler, among others, exhorts us these days not to give up one set of feelings for another, but to learn to feel more, to be able to tolerate a more and more complex emotional reality. Boynton and Dell's *Goodbye Mother, Hello Woman* offers us a practical guide to do exactly that.

—Anya Humphrey, Psychotherapist

This thoughtful book provides interesting and helpful structures to help women launch creative explorations of the mother-daughter bond.

—Thaisa Frank, author of *Desire,*
A Brief History of Camouflage, and
Enchanted Men.

DAUGHTERS SPEAK

"In understanding where Mother ends and we begin, we can retire Mother from her role of mothering and see her as another woman whom we may or may not like or love. Hence the title, *Goodbye Mother, Hello Woman*."

"The greatest loss of all is the loss of Mother, whether we felt mothered or not. The deepest grief is for the mothering we wanted and didn't receive."

"Finally, the time will come to say goodbye to Mother as Mother and to cut the emotional umbilical cord. Only then can we say hello to Mother as Woman."

"We can respect the ways we are different as well as affirm the ways we are the same."

"Growing up after age 30 is about choices, fulfillment, fruition, maturing and becoming whole."

"Some of us have been told, 'If it's good enough for your mother, it's good enough for you.' Accepting parents' values is not necessarily right for us."

"Taking a risk can bring surprises. Love can be released. A new and better relationship can be formed. Possibilities previously beyond our capacity to envision can open up."

"I want to tell you that I'm gay, that I feel like I've lived a lie most of my adult life. I want to share not only the pain of pretending, but also the joy of not pretending anymore."

"My mother's and my relationship was a result of how she reacted to *the boys*—my father and my brother. When she required a recruit to manage *the boys*, she created me—the dutiful daughter, the little hostess, the one who could never say no."

Goodbye Mother, Hello Woman

Goodbye Mother, Hello Woman

REWEAVING THE DAUGHTER MOTHER RELATIONSHIP

by

Marilyn Irwin Boynton, R.N., M.Ed.
and
Mary Dell, A. R. C. T., M. A.

NEW HARBINGER PUBLICATIONS, INC.

Publisher's Note

This publication is designed to provide accurate and authoritative information in regard to the subject matter covered. It is sold with the understanding that the publisher is not engaged in rendering psychological, financial, legal, or other professional services. If expert assistance or counseling is needed, the services of a competent professional should be sought.

Copyright ©1995 New Harbinger Publications, Inc.

5674 Shattuck Avenue

Oakland, CA 94609

Distributed in U.S.A. primarily by Publishers Group West; in Canada by Raincoast Books; in Great Britain by Airlift Book Company, Ltd.; in South Africa by Real Books, Ltd.; in Australia by Boobook; and in New Zealand by Tandem Press.

ISBN 1-57224-025-3 hardcover
ISBN 1-57224-024-5 paperback

Library of Congress Catalog Card Number: 95-69479

Originally published by Daughter Mother Press, Toronto, Ontario, Canada

Edited by Val Dumond
Cover Design by Lori Dell
Text Illustrations by Shauna Rae

First printing 1995, 8,000 copies
Second printing 1995, 7,000 copies

DEDICATION

This book is dedicated to the many women who so generously shared their personal stories with us and who we will never forget.

And to Marilyn's baby granddaughter, Emma Mary, and to her grandsons Kyle and Ryan, all of whom are our future.

And to Mary's grandsons, Boston, Matthew, Sachi and Nathan.

NOTES TO THE READER

This authors make the following suggestions when using this book:

√ A trustworthy therapist is recommended.

√ Page through the book to get a flavour of the material, then work through each chapter one by one.

√ Take time to absorb the ideas and experience the activities.

√ Keep a journal. Writing a small amount each day provides a valuable overall picture of your journey.

√ Expect to cry. Tears are part of the healing process.

√ Find a three-ring notebook with pages of plastic pockets to store meaningful mementoes, such as dress scraps, locks of hair, buttons, old lace, pressed flowers, earrings, shells and photos. In it, note your visualizations, dreams, symbols, memories, insights and choices for change in your life.

CONTENTS

IN GRATITUDE

Both authors wish to express their special thanks to a number of people who supported this project and helped make it possible: Donald Williamson, Val Dumond, Anya Humphrey, Victor Dell, Franca Leeson, Shauna Rae and Barbara Pressman.

Mary Dell offers a special thanks to...
...her four daughters, Elizabeth, Christina, Cynthia, and Lorraine;
...her mother, Edith, and to her grandmother, Mary Jane;
...and to all the wise grandmothers who have gone before.

Marilyn Boynton extends thanks to...
"...My children, Christopher, John, and Mary, who believed in me, and who never lost faith in their mother's ability to realize a lifelong ambition;
"...My husband, Lindsey Wellner;
"...My friends and family who patiently listened to me relate the countless little heartbreaks that go into writing a book like this one.
"...To my mother, Beatrice Isabel, now deceased, who stood by me and was available for me to do my work with her."

FOREWORD

Bravo! What delightful reading. Marilyn Boynton and Mary Dell, both experienced women family therapists, have created a terrific book specifically for women, many of whom are "mothers" but all of whom are of course "daughters."

Their background interest is in "the threads of female bonding" from birth to death. They use this metaframe to explore what it means to be female at this time in this culture. But their central theme is what they believe to be the universal challenge to all women—to transform daughterhood into womanhood. So this is a book about intergenerational relationships.

Intergenerational relationships do of course include men. But Marilyn and Mary have chosen to isolate and highlight that part of the family system which is the relationship between mother and daughter. Their particular goal is to help women (daughters) who feel psychologically "stuck" in relationships with their mother, and who are consequently blocked in many other aspects of their lives as well. The authors propose that struggles with a mate, boss or sister may result from projections onto them of unresolved personal relationship issues with mothers.

The challenge—and the solution as they see it—is to be able to say goodbye to Mother in her role of "mommy," and hello to the now aging woman behind the mother role. It is a most worthy goal.

The argument builds on two assumptions. First is the assumption that every daughter is in some way tied to the mother of the past, and would like to change the arrangement. The authors suggest that by taking personal responsibility for one's own well-being in life, a woman can learn to mother herself. As a consequence, a daughter can then approach Mother woman-to-woman, thereby seeing her as an equal. This is the heart of the argument of the book, and it is a very good heart.

The second assumption is that the deepest grief which any woman can experience in life has to do with the nurturing mothering which she did not receive. As a consequence, mothers who were not themselves well mothered will expect their daughters to mother them.

In regard to this core grief, the authors say, welcome your tears and grieve. Then you can release Mother as a mother and claim your own power. This is of course long-term work and this book serves as a clear and concise guide for adult women on their journeys to personal freedom.

This is a book which could (and probably should) only be written by women for women. It expresses a view which can come only from inside a woman's perspective, only from women who have themselves done their own work. The authors are women who know what it means both to be Daughter and to be Mother, and beyond this who have guided many women on the journey.

They grasp the essential dilemma of intergenerational relationships, which I have named *The Intimacy Paradox*. How does one define clear boundaries to the self, transcending the remarkable power of family emotionality, and simultaneously celebrate belongingness with one's own flesh and blood? What is most appealing in response to this question is that Mary and Marilyn temper their understanding of individuation with an appreciation of the powerful (if often conflicted) biologically-grounded bonding—and sometimes bondage—between the generations.

This dilemma cannot be resolved unilaterally nor by tantrums. The adult management of the challenge is itself the most compelling evidence of a good outcome. Personal freedom is not freedom from intergenerational connection but rather freedom of choice within it. So Marilyn and Mary write with an empathy and a compassion which honors the struggles of both generations of women, and they support "a balance of fairness."

That is why it is such a treat for me to write this foreword. This is what makes this practical guidebook so effective. While sensitive to the older generation, they support the emotional emancipation of women within the families into which they have been born as daughters.

The reader will be enlightened and motivated—and moved by the story.

Donald S. Williamson, Ph.D.
Leadership Institute of Seattle
June 1994

INTRODUCTION

The story of Demeter and Persephone is the earliest known story of a daughter and mother. This Greek legend, threading its way throughout this book, is a classic example of a daughter becoming her own person with Mother.

DEMETER/PERSEPHONE

An ancient daughter and mother story tells about Persephone and Demeter —Demeter, the Grain-Mother, the giver of crops, and Persephone, her daughter, the Grain-Maiden who symbolizes the new crop. This tale pre-dates Homer's *Hymn to Demeter* written around the seventh century BC, and certainly existed long before the Judeo-Christian deification of father and son. Originally Demeter was seen as both mother and daughter simultaneously. It was later that the maiden became a separate entity known as the daughter Persephone.

Demeter's name comes from that time when they were worshipped as one goddess; the dead were called Demetreioi, "Demeter's people." Not only did she bring all things to life but she received them back into her bosom at death. Demeter represented life restored.

There are many versions of her story. In one, Demeter teaches mortals to plant, cultivate, harvest and store grains. This task was entrusted to women early in our civilisation with the belief that the fecundity of the womb is transferred to the fields of grain through female hands.

As the legend unfolds, Persephone asks her mother about the spirits of the dead she sometimes encounters. Demeter explains, "I instruct mortals to store their grain in pits under the earth where the spirits of the dead will fertilize the seed. Then

I draw up the crops from below, to the surface of the earth to feed the living."

When Persephone announces her choice as a goddess is to care for the souls of the dead, Demeter is shocked. She does not want her beloved daughter to live in the dark gloom of the underworld. Finally, however, she accepts Persephone's decision: "You are loving and giving. We cannot give to ourselves only; you must go. But for every day that you remain in the underworld I will grieve for your absence."

So Persephone takes three poppies and three sheaves of wheat on her trip. Demeter lights a torch for her to find the way. As Persephone descends, she holds the sheaves close to her heart. Coming into an enormous cavern where the spirits of the dead reside, she arranges an altar on a large, flat rock. There is a stand for her torch, a vase for the wheat, and a bowl of pomegranate seeds which are the food of the dead.

Inviting these souls to come before her, she embraces them one by one, gazes into their eyes, and paints their foreheads with the red juice of the pomegranate as she chants:

"You have waxed into the fullness of life

And waned into darkness;

May you be renewed in tranquility and wisdom."

While Persephone receives and renews the spirits in the underworld, Demeter remains disconsolate. In her sorrow, she withdraws her power from the crops and the fields are barren. A cold dark pall hangs over the earth.

One morning Demeter sees a ring of crocus break through the earth. A warm breeze sings, "Persephone returns! Persephone returns!" As her daughter ascends from a deep cavern, Demeter throws a handmade cape of white crocus around her daughter's shoulders. They cry and laugh and hug and dance.

Even today, every winter we mourn with Demeter her daughter's absence, and every spring we rejoice in Persephone's return.

This ancient legend could be viewed as the earliest story of female individuation, which means becoming our own unique selves. This is our inner journey, which we cannot do by ourselves. Like Persephone seeking information from her mother about the underworld, we often begin by remembering our past—our mothers' and grandmothers' history. We go home sometime after age thirty to ask the questions we've never dared ask.

THE UNKNOWN SELF

At some point we come to the dark void, or empty place, the unknown where only we can go. The child in us has the faith, the innocence and the curiosity to lead us on. The mother in us may go unwillingly, fearfully, sorrowfully into this unlit, unfamiliar place within—the unknown self.

On this stage of the journey we may want to withdraw from social involvement, from outer life. We may spend hours in inner reflection. Perhaps we cry more than we think we ought. We may feel too tired to push ourselves into the business of life and of accomplishing tasks. Like Demeter we are waiting for our daughter-self to return. We "contemplate our navels"— which symbolizes the place of descent into the underworld, our unconscious. We are waiting for our energy to return. It is this energy that motivates us to expand, to take action, to create.

In our society we are more comfortable with *doing*. Certainly this is how we gain recognition for our accomplishments. When we remain in this *doing* mode for a long time, others' approval becomes too important—it runs our lives. Sometimes we need to rest, to contract, to be in touch with the core of our being rather than our doing.

Most of us are trained when young to nurture others. We

may not recognize for many years that we have lost our child selves. An inner wisdom guides us in finding ourselves again. We also need external guides who become the torch that lights our way. For while we want to become who we can be, we also don't want to change. We fear the unfamiliar. Real life guides can support our descent to the underworld, and our ascent to the upper world again.

Persephone's poppies put her to sleep—they taught her how to go into a trance to reach her unconscious. The sheaves of wheat she carried near her heart reminded her of her mother's love; they helped her "feed" herself. The torch lighting her way is symbolic of people who have gone before.

When we ascend we are different than before. We are expanded. We are more of ourselves. As the Demeter and Persephone parts of ourselves unite, we become more powerful and more creative in our lives.

A Journey Worth Taking

When we are little, we depend on our mothers to take care of us, to protect us, to love us. When we grow up, we often find it difficult to get past depending on Mother for that care. She may have died. She may live far away. Still, we find ourselves performing to please her, longing for her approval, wishing desperately for her love.

To make matters more complex, we often don't know that we're still trying to please Mom. We think we're trying to please a husband, the boss, neighbours, a teacher, friends. It may seem like we're doing battle with ourselves and we may become ill with our feelings of *dis-ease*. We may feel hardpressed to explain what ails us.

In all probability, we have never shifted our relationship with Mother to a more grownup level. We have never released Mother from taking care of us, from treating us as children. We may never have released ourselves from taking care of Mother and trying to earn her love. The professionals call this release process *individuation*. This means becoming independent and relating as adults.

Individuation is a lifetime journey; it means becoming who we are.

As children we were little and helpless and parents were big and in control. They had the power. It isn't until our 30s or 40s that we are ready to equalize this power. It's Daughter's work. It's conscious work. We know we're doing it when we can be ourselves with authority figures; when we can see them as equal persons rather than having power over us; when we feel that we neither have to please nor rebel against them; when our relationships are neither dependent nor independent but more interdependent.

A common theme for women engaged in this individuation process is the search for a medium through which to express the essence of who we are. In reclaiming and integrating the lost, or undeveloped, parts of ourselves, we need to look for a way of being that is most congruent for us as a whole person. Our unique selves unfold in an organic rhythm as we learn to trust this journey into our inner world.

All women are daughters. Some of us are still tied securely to our mothers; some wish we were closer to our mothers; some of us regret not getting to know our mothers. Some would like to have nothing more to do with our mothers. Some of us have never known our mothers; some grew up with surrogate mothers, step-mothers, aunts, grandmothers. Still, we all are tied to the mother of our past.

In the past, individuation was taken to mean leaving Mother behind, getting away from her, getting out of her life. Now we know that to separate from Mother doesn't mean to stop loving her, or even being with her. It only means to stop expecting her to take care of us.

Daughters All

Our inheritances as daughters are the positive and negative messages we received from our families when we were children—the pleasant and painful memories of past events, the beliefs and behaviours passed down from one generation to another, the nurturing or non-nurturing we received, the feelings we denied or experienced about these life events.

This book helps us remember and re-experience in a new way our relationship with that central person in our lives (whether we loved or hated her)—Mother.

Goodbye Mother, Hello Woman is a guide for changing our relationship with Mother. Each chapter describes the steps used to cut the emotional umbilical cord. They suggest ways to begin to defuse some of the intense emotion that exists between daughters and mothers. One way is to ask questions about family traditions, loyalties and secrets.

Throughout the book clients and friends have generously shared their stories to illustrate this process. The authors also share their own connections with their mothers. In visualizing their connections with their own mothers, Mary Dell's takes the form of violets; Marilyn Boynton's is in the shape of pansies.

Mary's Story

A long time ago I dreamed of my mother standing in the shade of one of the big maples that stood like guardians across the front lawn of our old farmhouse. Their roots made caves, roads, bridges and pools when it rained, where the fairies lived. Violets grew in the ditch between them and the road beyond. I visited them often, when I was little.

In my dream, the hot summer day was covered with a bluebird-coloured sky and cumulus clouds. My mother wore a violet dress trimmed with the hand-crocheted lace she loved and a wide-brimmed hat, although in real life she didn't like wide brims. She was smiling at me.

That dream is as clear today as when I dreamed it. Such a web of connections existed between my mother and me. It has taken a lifetime to separate her colours and patterns from mine and create my own. Early in life, I learned to imitate her; in my teens and 20s, I did the exact opposite—nothing she did was right for me.

My mother wrote as a way of expressing herself. Earlier in my life I wanted to be a writer, but studied music instead. Now at age 65 I am returning to the road not taken. Writing is also a way for me to express who I am under the masks of daughter, wife, mother, grandmother and professional.

In my heart, my mother and violets are intertwined, just as she and I are. Every spring my front yard is full of violets. I am my mother's daughter. I am my own person.

Marilyn's Story

Ojai, California was where it happened; that was where I got my first clue that confirmed the value of my work with daughters and mothers. My co-author and I, both family therapists, were attending a professional conference. Our accommodations were a Bed and Breakfast managed by a mother and daughter team.

The first morning, our hosts joined us for tea after breakfast and the discussion led to shop talk about mothers and daughters—our favourite topic. The daughter proudly explained that the cups and saucers we held were hand-painted by her mother. It was then Mary noticed that her cup and saucer were trimmed with violets, her mother's flower. I noticed I held a cup and saucer different from Mary's. In my hand was a teacup painted with the glorious colours of pansies.

At that very moment I realized how pansies represented a deep connection with my mother. I remembered how it had been a delightful daily task for me to pick bunches of pansies from the rock garden for her. I remembered how I would float each one carefully in a crystal bowl and then we would admire their fragile loveliness together.

Sitting in that sunlit California dining room, I knew I had been handed certain cards to play out. In the 12 years that followed, Mary and I wrote and re-wrote, and conducted workshops about and for daughters and mothers. From these women, I garnered a body of experiences which have blossomed into this book. Fathoming the mysteries between daughters and mothers has become a life work for me.

Goodbye Mother, Hello Woman lifts the veil on the love-hate relationship between adult daughters and mothers and allows us to shift the focus to knowing each other as women. The first step is to get to know the little girl we once were. The next step is to look at where we came from, who our grandparents and great-grandparents were. Only then can we take a look at Mother and begin to see her as the child of her parents, a person who had her own hopes and dreams for her life.

We'll start the journey the same way all important journeys begin: by preparing, by doing our homework, and by sorting out Grandmother's things—her dreams, her desires, her losses, her treasures. Then we'll move on to Mother and her keepsakes.

In learning how we relate to Mother, perhaps as a clinging vine or as a disinterested stranger, we are able to uncover the feelings that were once strong and now may be submerged somewhere deep inside. We'll take time to cry. Tears are a natural and necessary response to loss. When we suffer any kind of loss, the pain of all other losses somehow is summoned. A loss need not be a thing or a person; it could be the loss of a stage in life, the loss of a habit, or the loss of a moment. Every loss, no matter how insignificant it may seem on the surface, still becomes a trigger to recall the earlier pain.

The greatest loss of all is the loss of Mother, whether we felt mothered or not. The deepest grief is for the mothering we wanted and didn't receive. The shedding of tears acts like a salve to attend to this grief and begin the healing. Don't hold back the tears. Let them fall, for they are a source of renewal. An old saying claims that tears cleanse the eyes so they can see more clearly.

Finally, the time will come to say goodbye to Mother as Mother, to let go of the feelings that restrict us, to untie the cord that binds us. Only then can we take back our power as a woman and welcome Mother to join us. Only then can we say hello to Mother as Woman.

CHAPTER 1

In the ancient story of Demeter and Persephone, Demeter gives her daughter a torch, three sheaves of wheat, and three poppies—symbols of light, nourishment and enlightenment. They strengthen Persephone on her journey into the underworld. In this book women share their stories with voices that encourage, support and exhort us never to give up on ourselves. We are not alone!

1

GETTING TO KNOW OURSELVES

Perhaps what life is all about is becoming who we are. The theme of this book is individuation, focusing on the daughter mother dyad. Most often it takes a crisis to create change—a loss through death, divorce, a child leaving home, or being fired from a job. Whether we know it or not, struggles with a mate, boss or sister are often projections of our primal relationship with Mother—the relationship which holds the most love and pain for us.

Recently a friend complained about the word individuate. "It suggests separation, but it leaves out our connectedness to the human experience," she said. Some of the other phrases women use for this work: *a sorting-out time, learning to bear the full weight of my own existence, snipping the restraining wires on a stunted bonsai plant.* Some people describe it as *an inner journey, staying in a relationship with a significant other while separating from them,* or *weaving together life threads that have been lost or damaged.* The words and images may be different but the process for individuating is the same. It involves increasing, not decreasing, our connectedness to human experience while we grow.

This is different for each person, there are no maps showing where to start, where to go, or how to do it. It is not a straight path from here to there, but rather a continuous spiral down into our inner core. It is going into the unknown, requiring faith in our own wisdom that comes from a wisdom greater than our own.

Dreaming can be an inspiration for this work, with symbols as metaphors to light the way. A *grandmother* dream almost certainly announces the beginning of the descent into our underworld. Here is a dream of a young woman entering therapy.

Ursula's Story

I dreamed I was looking for something in my grandmother's basement—old cookie cutters and baking pans for a church rummage sale. While looking through the musty cupboards, I discovered some old treasures, which excited me. Among them was a large, black, heart-shaped cloisonné box with gold trim and coloured flowers on it. I felt the expectation that it held something very importantt. Then I woke up.

On the next visit to my therapist, I told her how furious I felt that I hadn't been able to see what was inside the box. With her help, I returned to the dream and saw the box. Breathlessly I opened the lid. I could clearly see two small objects—an acorn and the skeleton of a tiny animal. I burst into tears, shocked and disappointed. I had expected a magic key to the meaning of life.

We worked on the dream. As a child of about six, I remembered how delighted I was when my father showed me a nest of baby squirrels. He put them in a small box for me and allowed me to play with them; they seemed like living dolls.

But they didn't act like my dolls. They wiggled and squirmed and had minds of their own. I did what I knew parents were supposed to do; I punished them. Even now I cry when I remember calling them naughty and spanking one for trampling another. My father discovered me and took the squirrels away. I felt very ashamed.

While I felt I had done something bad, I was also confused about why it was all right for my father to spank my baby brother but not right for me to spank the squirrel.

The image of the tiny squirrel skeleton had literally opened a skeleton in my closet. I carry a heritage of abuse; my parents thought babies became good by cruel spankings.

The acorn? My mother's maiden name means "oak twig." The family even had jewelry designed with oak leaves and acorns. The acorn in the box felt like hope for me, a promise that I can plant a new tree with my life. I can help others live better, happier lives. Isn't it interesting that acorns are nourishment for squirrels?

The two objects in the box of my dream represent for me my real inheritance, shame and hope. I got what I wanted from the box after all.

Joan's Story

Joan, a charming, successful professional tells about her journey.

My mother didn't like babies. I grew up learning that people who liked babies were weak-minded. Intelligent people preferred children when they were "older, and more interesting." My mother proudly states that I was never a child. I bathed myself at two and at ten I was reading Overstreet's The Mature Mind.

My mother used to tell me not to count on her as a grandmother— and I never did. I knew how much she didn't enjoy children, so at age 28 I had a tubal ligation. I was confident I never wanted to have children.

My mother is very childlike, and it is clear to me now that she wants to be the only child. Only a few months ago I recognized an event in her childhood that I surmise prevented her from growing up. I was finally able to accept the reality of my mother as developmentally arrested at nine years old.

I learned to be ashamed of being a child and being a female. In retrospect I see myself as a bonsai plant, contorted to meet the needs and ideals of my parents. I was wired from the inside to be a sexually attractive, geisha-style, never pregnant woman. I earned a man-sized income with man-sized responsibility. My mother was proud of me.

Though I do not think of my mother as willfully malicious, I never could understand her inability to see my needs and care for me. As I mourn my loss of being a child and my loss of being a mother, and as I work to recover my pride of womanhood, I know I am on my own…that is, I am motherless.

Part of my individuation is to see my mother as toxic to me—the biochemical sensation is very real. I remember writing a poem once—"Venom, thy name is Mother." Her poison bonsai'd me, but now I can sniff the poison and I can refuse to drink.

If I play with the bonsai metaphor, I see the individuation process as snipping the constraining wires, and re-potting myself. I may have been a perfectly adapted little creature—conveniently nice for everyone at home and at work—but I was stunted.

To nurture myself simply for the joy of it is my inner journey. In this work I am taking my cues from dreams, stories, body tensions and pain. I am tired of trying to seduce the world. On an aptitude test in school I exceeded the female scale for 'ability to sell.' I am tired of trying to please, cajole, mediate, manipulate, facilitate. I realize that my infancy was the first great sales task: to make my parents accept a baby in the house. I had to be as little like a child/ baby/female as possible.

Now I don't need to reach out and try to get my mother to finally see the baby. The baby is now mine. I will nurture her with the passion of any mother.

A recent dream suggests I've been living in one small, beautiful room in a house that has many huge, wonderful, empty rooms. The rooms both scare me and invite me. The house is part of my journey, and this journey is worth my life!

Up until now, Joan's role in life has been to mother her mother. Mothers who themselves were not mothered when they were children unconsciously expect their daughters to give them what they missed growing up.

Afraid of passing on her mothering deprivation to the next generation, Joan chose an abortion at age 18, and a tubal ligation at 28. Now, at this point in her life, she is ready to give up hoping her mother will finally see her motherlessness. She has accepted that she will have to mother herself. In order to do this, she first must terminate her role of mothering Mother, although this does not mean she will stop loving her mother.

Joan has accepted the pain of her childhood, and is discovering the joy of being. She knows she has the inner strength and resources to take full responsibility for her life. Perhaps the more difficult task will be to ask for, and accept, caring from other women.

Emily's Story

Emily, a middle-aged woman who is a caring and supportive wife and mother while developing her own career, tells a different tale.

I was born in England just before the outbreak of the second World War. In spite of difficult times, I always knew that I was wanted and loved. I have seen photographs of my mother and me together, and she read some of her journals to me. One line stands out: after describing me physically, she wrote "I adore her!"

My mother had to bring us up alone in those early years, with my father away in the air force. I saw her as strong, capable, serene, beautiful and deeply religious. In spite of enemy planes, the blackout, bombs falling nearby and food rationing, I never felt afraid. To me, this was normal life. I was secure in my mother's love and care.

Love of the arts and culture were very much a part of my life— trips to London for a play, ballet or symphony concert, regular visits to the library, gifts of books on birthdays and at Christmas. My mother was a writer and affirmed my own writing, though she didn't ask to see my work or to share my feelings. I had a lot of privacy. I often roamed the countryside alone.

It wasn't until much later in my life that I became aware of how desperately I wanted intimacy. When my mother told me a few years ago that I needed to be alone a lot as a child, I wondered if I'd had a choice. I was a good girl and I longed to please her. She needed her solitude and privacy, so I was taught I had the same needs. I had no quarrel with that at the time. I loved my fantasy world; I didn't miss sharing it. I was basically content.

My mother and father gave me a model of almost movie star, happily-ever-after togetherness. My father, a newspaper man after the war, encouraged Mother in her writing. My mother, with her deep faith, encouraged my father in his lay preaching on weekends. Their styles and talents were very different but highly complementary. As well as being lovers, they were friends and colleagues.

Where did I fit in? In retrospect, it's clear to me that while I was wanted, I don't think I ever felt needed. Ironically, now that my mother is elderly and quite incapacitated, she needs me to help her in very basic ways. I know my being and presence are valued, yet there is still a nagging feeling that real intimacy is not there. Sadly, it may be too late. There is still a longing to share all my feelings, to be truly accepted as I am, not just for the image of the ideal daughter. I realize, with some sadness, that I have carried on these patterns with my children. I long to be close, open, and honest, but often feel incapable. I don't ask them personal questions, but as my mother did, I wait, hoping they know I'm here and I care.

While my parents gave me the best of everything, I received their subtle prejudices. People, books, and films that weren't up to their standards were "beneath us," and to be avoided at all costs. There were enormous unspoken expectations. Great importance was placed on goodness, politeness, and obedience. I picked up all the typical injunctions put on most girls, with the added baggage of being "English" and "Christian."

The down side of all this is my complete inability to deal with anger. Not only did it take me years to recognize it in myself, I also have an unrealistic fear of it in others. To a degree, this blocks my straightforward expression of other feelings. I long to break out of this restriction, but have had little success, even with helpful therapists.

My mother would (I presume) be surprised and shocked by the amount of professional help I have sought. I imagine she would see it as a failure on her part. I don't wish that. I take full responsibility for my life. At the same time, I recognize a lot of injunctions to be the perfect child and woman, one that would reflect well on my parents.

Yes, I do have a lot of anger, a lot of denial, but for the most part, much love.

Unlike Joan, Emily had an adult parent who protected and cared for her physically and mentally, but was not available emotionally. Both mothers needed their daughters to look good, to be good, "to reflect well on them." Both daughters long for more feelings—their own as well as their mothers'—for more intimacy, for more sharing.

Emily's mother and father seemed to form a self-sufficient couple. They protected their child from their adult feelings. Many people believe children do not have feelings, ignoring and denying them as non-existent. It seems possible that these parents didn't shift roles from being parents to being people with their adult children.

In Emily's family, her parents may have unconsciously felt that the expression of emotions was "beneath them." Protecting Emily may have been a way to protect themselves from their own feelings and the fear of expressing them. Not showing feelings can be a legacy passed down for generations. Emily knows she is continuing this pattern with her own children.

WHO AM I?

Looking backwards to where we came from is a beginning. Whether we inherited a functional or dysfunctional family, we can still discover who we are within this system. Which family legacies are helpful or harmful? How are these inheritances stumbling blocks? How can they be transformed to help?

When we realize we have nothing to lose and everything to gain by searching for the lost parts of ourselves, we can stop blaming Mother. We can become blame-free. Discovering the truth becomes fact finding, not fault finding.

In this book, several kinds of tools are described with instructions to help find facts: family maps, genograms, feelings, blocking messages, empowering messages, *herlooms*, and suggestions for steps to take in equalizing the power.

In understanding where Mother ends and we begin, we can retire Mother from her role of mothering and see her as another woman whom we may or may not like, or love. Hence the title: *Goodbye Mother, Hello Woman*. We can respect the ways in which we are different as well as affirm the ways we are the same. This is a long and often painful and frightening journey, but as Joan exclaims, "This journey is worth my life!"

GUIDELINES

Reflecting

- What have I learned from the crises in my life?

- Is there something in my life I need to give up?

- What's stopping me from doing what I need to do?

- What is one change I am willing to make?

- What am I not willing to do?

HIGHLIGHTS

- When we stop blaming Mother, we can focus on ourselves.

- Do fact-finding, not fault-finding.

- Behind the Mother mask is a woman.

- Respect how we are the same and how we are different.

- Roles need shifting; one of these is to retire Mother.

CHAPTER 2

Like Persephone, many of us are curious about our own underworld where we have stored feelings, memories and experiences. They are the seeds of renewal. In sorting them out we may discover family secrets we didn't know existed. We may find some powerful women whose spirits will encourage us to stand in our own power.

2

GETTING TO
KNOW
OUR ROOTS

Growing up after age 30 is about choices, fulfillment, fruition, maturing, and becoming whole. Our parents were responsible for our lives when we were small children. Taking back this responsibility means retiring parents from their parental roles. We no longer need to be unquestionably loyal to our parents' choices, behaviours and values. Being disloyal to their rules creates the space and time to discover what our own choices are.

Some of us have been told, "If it's good enough for your mother, it's good enough for you." Accepting parents' values is not necessarily right for us. Our intuition is where the wisdom resides; this intuitive wisdom can tell us what is right. We are worth whatever time it takes to reconnect with this inner knowing.

In this chapter we introduce two tools that are useful in understanding the patterns of behaviour passed down through the generations. The first is a *family map*, which is like a candid snapshot. The second is a *genogram* which is simply an expanded family tree. It contains information about medical, professional, educational, psychological and spiritual family values.

Ellen's Story

For the last 20 years, Ellen, an astute businesswoman, has been climbing the corporate ladder. Here she describes what happened in her family before she was 12, how she felt about it then and how it is still affecting her life.

The person who is my adoptive mother was emotionally absent by the time I had arrived in her life. I was adopted at 15-days-old. Like many women of her generation, she existed only in the roles of Mum and Wife and Semi-Pro Do-Gooder. She was sensible and level-headed; she baked cookies for my friends and made beautiful Christmas decorations. She took me to Brownies and saw that I had piano and ballet lessons. I had a coat with a white fur collar. She certainly never hit me. All the other members of our somewhat eccentric family praised her "normalcy." In short, my mother was her role; she had read the Mother Manual.

Dad was a dysfunctional alcoholic, and a driven workaholic and very successful in business. He just roared through life like some force of nature, rolling over anyone in his path and creating chaos all around him. There was no room for anyone in his life.

My brother was a "bad" kid with behaviour problems. He was banished to boarding school: one wild card at home was enough for my mother.

The relationship between my mother and me really was the result of the way she reacted to "the boys"—my father and my brother. Strangely, the havoc they created in our lives was viewed rather benignly by her as "shenanigans." So when my mother required a recruit to manage the boys, she "created" me: the dutiful daughter, the little hostess, the one who could never say "no."

To help Ellen visualize and clarify her family system, she drew a simple map that showed at a glance how the family operated. See Diagram 1, Ellen's Family Map.

Ellen's Family Map

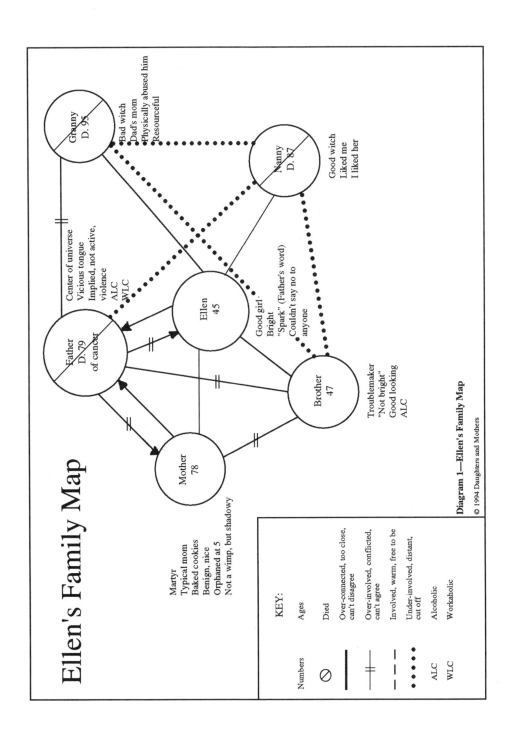

Diagram 1—Ellen's Family Map

© 1994 Daughters and Mothers

Then Ellen drew lines to connect members of her family, indicating the relationships that prevailed. She noticed immediately how the family formed triangular relationships. See Diagram 2.

Ellen's Family Map

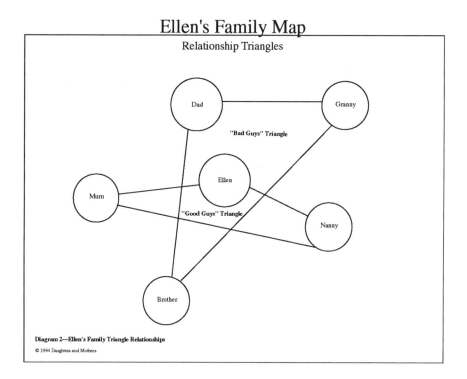

Relationship Triangles

Diagram 2—Ellen's Family Triangle Relationships

© 1994 Daughters and Mothers

TRIANGLES

In Ellen's family there are two obvious triangles—"The Good Guys" and "The Bad Guys."

By themselves, triangles are neither good nor bad; they are a fact of life. It's what we do with them that makes them either harmful or helpful. When triangulation becomes strangulation through inflexibility and rigidity, the relationship becomes dysfunctional. Stuckness is deadness.

A triangle is helpful when the roles and functions of the individuals shift frequently. This creates more freedom and energy.

The "good guys" and the "bad guys" are outstanding features of Ellen's family. Triangles in other families might be: the powerful and the helpless, the men and the women, or Mom's kids and Dad's kids. While the family system is non-negotiable as a child, adult children can and do make changes.

The major triangle in a family consists of Mother, Father and Child. Here are three variations of this configuration.

1) If one or both parents never grew up, the child becomes a surrogate parent.

2) When a parent leaves, whether by death or distance, intentional or unintentional, physical or emotional, this loss creates a vacuum in the family that one of the children fills—usually the most responsible one. Since young children are physically and emotionally available, this particular child probably also assumes the role of surrogate mate to some degree, even though she is too developmentally immature. Sometimes this child becomes a physically sexual partner; other times the relationship is an emotionally seductive one.

3) Another possibility is for the parents to create an impermeable boundary around their relationship that excludes the child.

While many permutations are possible, an adult child can discover and transform the roles in her family. This is the task in which Ellen is still engaged.

She describes how Mother created the dutiful daughter:

Mum constantly advised me how to defuse and distract my father. She merely suggested that I change what I was doing or saying or wearing to something more suitable. I was good at changing, learning from an early age to dance for Daddy and serve as Mummy's little domestic assistant. Interestingly, my brother was never asked to do domestic chores: no ironing, dishes or cleaning. I didn't even notice until much later, when I had left home. I just accepted this was woman's work.

The deeper reasons that made it so easy for Ellen to become the perfect geisha girl, as she sometimes calls herself, are clear:

I did everything she asked. I suspect being given away by my natural mother at birth set up in me an intense fear of abandonment, although I can only call it that in hindsight. I just always remember feeling extreme discomfort whenever anyone disapproved of me. With my father untouchable, and, I suspect, my brother wishing me dead, Mum was my only ally; her disapproval meant total isolation for me. She was good at it. She rarely raised her voice. She just slammed doors and froze me out for weeks. That was too hard to bear and too scary, so I always caved in.

Ellen's greatest fear is being abandoned and alone. This fear is not the result of an over-active imagination; it has real roots in her past. In her primal struggle to survive, she tries hard to be the best at pleasing. The price she pays is high:

I never really missed not having a personality until I was 30 or so, when I realized I didn't know who I was or what I wanted, unless someone requested a 'performance' of me. I became whatever anyone wanted me to be. I was getting tired. I felt the profound loneliness that comes from abandoning one's self. I was frantic and scared most of the time.

So I began, far away from the family, to look for myself—the little girl who was too frightened to be. It's a struggle. The old messages I learned at Mummy's knee —that I'm not good enough—die hard. I am addicted to the approval of others.

As for my mother, she played her role so long that when it was no longer required, she quite literally lost her mind. It seems she had given up any notion of her self so long ago that, when her duties were finished, there was no self for her to come home to.

Presently, Ellen is facing the illusion that she has to continue to please to ensure her survival. The truth is: she has survived! She is choosing not to be a martyr like mother, or a narcissist like father. After quitting an unfulfilling job, she is getting to know herself. She reflects:

I'd like to say that I've experienced some sort of revolution within that kept me, and continues to keep me, out of my mother's shoes, but it isn't true.

I realized as I grew older that my mother was a drudge who, for all her compliance, got treated badly. She was not loved, touched, or treated with respect by her husband or son. It doesn't take much of a leap of intellect to ascertain that this is not a good way to live, however much praise you get from the outside world for being a saint. There is just no payoff.

I suppose I should resent all my lost youth, slaving over a hot iron or dusting on Saturdays while my brother played, but in a way I am grateful that my mother provided such a negative role model. I don't want to be a drudge like Mum, and there is a lot of support for me to reject her values and go my own way.

We can be disloyal to our parents' values and still value our parents as people. There is a difference between valuing and loving, however. Digging up the past may seem to threaten the love in our relationships. If we are no longer dutiful or loyal, will there still be love in our hearts? If love is there, it will only become stronger. More often we choose the familiar, even if we don't like it, rather than risk the unfamiliar. Venturing into the unknown is a risk.

Taking a risk can bring surprises. Love can be released. A new and better relationship can be formed. Possibilities previously beyond our capacity to envision can open up.

GENOGRAMS

Drawing a genogram is a way of researching the history of your family of origin. It is more comprehensive than a family map, more like a posed family portrait. For years, family historians have gathered material for family trees. A similar tool is a family genogram, a drawing of three or more generations. Patterns of behaviours in each successive generation will be visible. Knowing they exist gives us the choice to change or retain them.

This research will stir up memories and raise questions about other family members' experiences, as well as our own. Putting a wide-angle lens on the camera for an intergenerational portrait defuses the intensity of feelings that overwhelmed us as children. Shameful secrets as well as unexpected gifts are likely to be uncovered. These are then available for integration that brings wholeness. Bringing to light hidden material also releases blocked energy—energy we can use to achieve desired goals.

Marcia's genogram is shown (Diagram 3) to illustrate the various pieces of information to collect. She further broke down her genogram into separate illustrations of relationships on her mother's side of the family and on her father's side. (See Diagrams 4 and 5.)

Marcia's Genogram

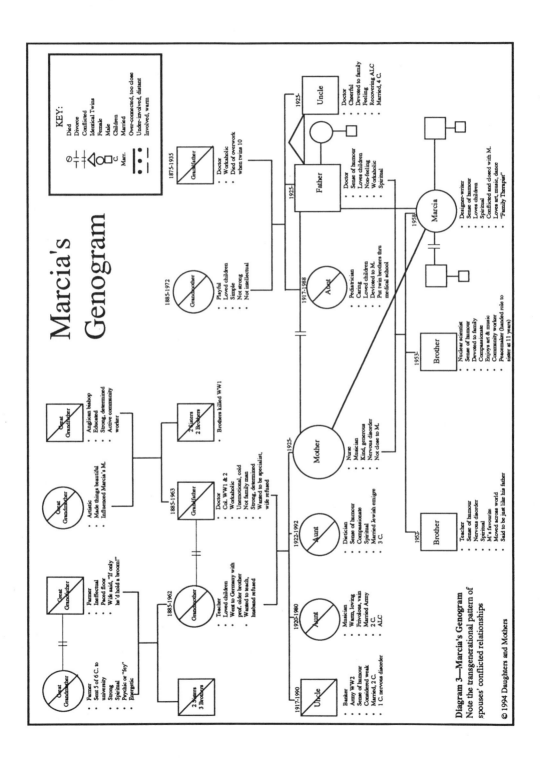

KEY:

⊘	Died
‡	Divorce
⋀	Conflicted
△	Identical Twins
○	Female
□	Male
C.	Children
Marr.	Married
⋯	Over-connected, too close
---	Under-involved, distant
───	Involved, warm

Great Grandfather
- Farmer
- Ineffectual
- Paced floor
- Wife said, "If only he'd hold a broom!"

Great Grandmother
- Seat 5 of 6 C. to university
- Strong
- Spiritual
- Psychic or "fey"
- Energetic

2 Sisters
3 Brothers

Uncle 1917-1990
- Banker
- Army WW2
- Sense of humour
- Considered weak
- Married, 2 C.
- 1 C. nervous disorder

Great Grandfather
- Artistic
- Made things beautiful
- Influenced Marcia's M.

Grandfather 1885-1963
- Doctor
- Col, WW1 & 2
- Workaholic
- Unemotional, cold
- Not family man
- Strong, determined
- Wanted to be specialist, wife refused

Grandmother 1885-1962
- Teacher
- Loved children
- Went to Germany with prof, older brother
- Wanted to teach, husband refused

Aunt 1920-1980
- Musician
- Warm, loving
- Frivolous, vain
- Married Army
- 2 C.
- ALC

Aunt 1922-1992
- Dietician
- Sense of humour
- Compassionate
- Spiritual
- Married Jewish emigre
- 3 C.

Great Grandfather
- Anglican bishop
- Educated
- Strong, determined
- Active community worker

2 Sisters
2 Brothers
- Brothers killed WW1

Grandmother 1885-1972
- Playful
- Loved children
- Simple
- Not strong
- Not intellectual

Grandfather 1875-1935
- Doctor
- Workaholic
- Died of overwork when twins 10

Mother 1925-
- Nurse
- Musician
- Kind, generous
- Nervous disorder
- Not close to M.

Father 1925-
- Doctor
- Sense of humour
- Loves children
- Non-feeling
- Spiritual
- Workaholic
- Spiritual

Uncle 1925-
- Doctor
- Cheerful
- Devoted to family
- Feeling
- Recovering ALC
- Married, 4 C.

Aunt 1917-1988
- Pediatrician
- Caring
- Loved children
- Devoted to M.
- Put twin brothers thru medical school

Brother 1952-
- Teacher
- Sense of humour
- Nervous disorder
- Spiritual
- M's favourite
- Moved across world
- Said to be just like his father

Brother 1953-
- Nuclear scientist
- Sense of humour
- Devoted to family
- Compassionate
- Enjoys art & music
- Community worker
- Peacemaker (handed role to sister at 11 years)

Marcia 1958-
- Designer-writer
- Sense of humour
- Loves children
- Spiritual
- Conflicted and closed with M.
- Loves art, music, dance
- "Family Therapist"

Diagram 3—Marcia's Genogram
Note the transgenerational pattern of spouses' conflicted relationships

© 1994 Daughters and Mothers

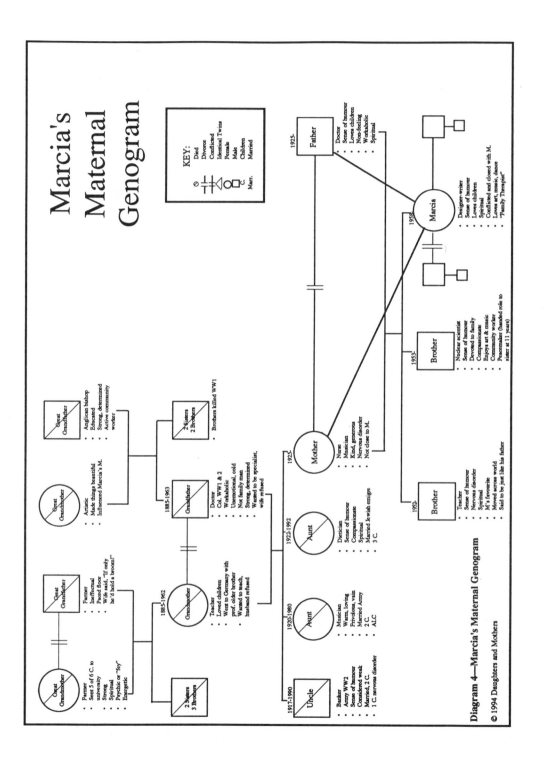

Marcia's Maternal Genogram

KEY:
- Died
- Divorce
- Conflicted
- Identical Twins
- Female
- Male
- Children
- Married
- Mar.

Great Grandmother
- Farmer
- Sent 5 of 6 C. to university
- Strong
- Spiritual
- Psychic or "fey"
- Energetic

Great Grandfather
- Farmer
- Ineffectual
- Paced floor
- Wife said, "If only he'd hold a broom!"

Great Grandmother
- Artistic
- Made things beautiful
- Influenced Marcia's M.

Great Grandfather
- Anglican bishop
- Educated
- Strong, determined
- Active community worker

2 Sisters 3 Brothers

Grandmother (1885-1962)
- Teacher
- Loved children
- Went to Germany with prof. older brother
- Wanted to teach, husband refused

Grandfather (1885-1963)
- Doctor
- Col. WW1 & 2
- Workaholic
- Unemotional, cold
- Not family man
- Strong, determined
- Wanted to be specialist, wife refused

2 Sisters 2 Brothers
- Brothers killed WW1

Uncle (1917-1990)
- Banker
- Army WW2
- Sense of humour
- Considered weak
- Married, 2 C.
- 1 C. nervous disorder

Aunt (1920-1980)
- Musician
- Warm, loving
- Frivolous, vain
- Married Army
- 2 C.
- ALC

Aunt (1922-1992)
- Dietician
- Sense of humour
- Compassionate
- Spiritual
- Married Jewish emigre
- 3 C.

Mother (1925)
- Nurse
- Musician
- Kind, generous
- Nervous disorder
- Not close to M.

Father (1925)
- Doctor
- Sense of humour
- Loves children
- Non-feeling
- Workaholic
- Spiritual

Brother (1953)
- Nuclear scientist
- Sense of humour
- Devoted to family
- Compassionate
- Enjoys art & music
- Community worker
- Peacemaker (handed role to sister at 11 years)

Brother (1955)
- Teacher
- Sense of humour
- Nervous disorder
- Spiritual
- M.'s favourite
- Moved across world
- Said to be just like his father

Marcia (1958)
- Designer-writer
- Sense of humour
- Loves children
- Spiritual
- Conflicted and closed with M.
- Loves art, music, dance
- "Family Therapist"

Diagram 4—Marcia's Maternal Genogram

© 1994 Daughters and Mothers

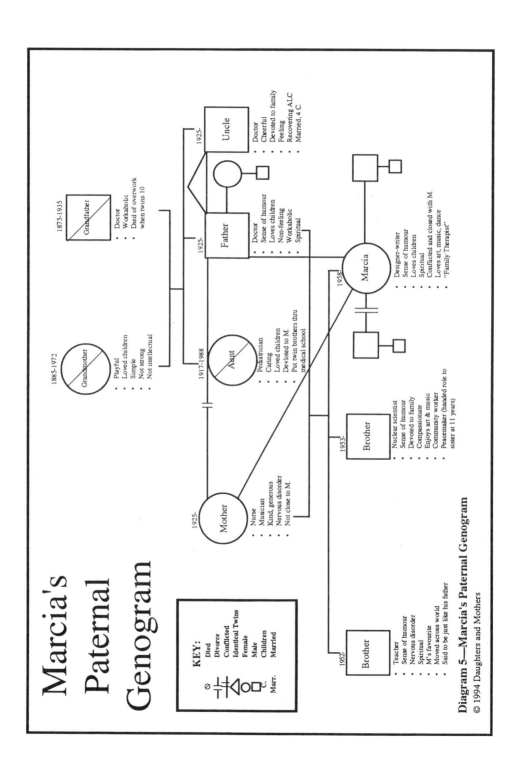

Diagram 5—Marcia's Paternal Genogram
© 1994 Daughters and Mothers

Marcia's Story

For Marcia, an intelligent and compassionate person, the search was initiated as a result of her mother's double bypass heart surgery followed by a psychotic episode. Since Marcia was the family "therapist," peacemaker, and Mom's caretaker, these were events of enough magnitude to rock Marcia's foundations. She has been asking questions and finding answers ever since. The following is a portion of what she has discovered in doing her genogram.

Certain themes jumped off the page of Marcia's drawing, values that occurred frequently on both sides of the family and between both sexes: sense of humour, spirituality, education, devotion to family, love of children, love of art and music, and nervous disorders. The men in both families tended to be workaholics, entered either medical or military professions and were often community workers.

The women tended to carry the artistic and musical talents and were often described as warm, compassionate and caring.

While the gender roles generally fit the traditional stereotypes, there were two striking exceptions: Mother's grandmother who was a farmer and sent five of her six children to university and Father's sister, a pediatrician, who put her twin brothers through medical school. Undoubtedly, these two women of the world have provided a strong legacy for Marcia and other family members, which is being passed on to their children.

In searching out these themes, Marcia used coloured pens to trace them through three and sometimes four generations. This helped put in perspective her mother's "nervous disorder" (as the family described it) and how it affected Marcia's life. She also discovered many vibrant and healthy influences.

The most notable dysfunction in her mother's family was the history of unresolved conflicts between spouses through the generations. This resulted in an over-involved relationship between Mom and the oldest son. Her grandparents' inability to respect each other's differences created two armed camps—Mom's kids and Dad's kids. Since we learn how to relate by watching our parents and believe what happens in our family is "normal," we re-create the same system in our own marriages. Marcia sees that the conflict between her mother and father is similar to her own pattern: she may be over-protective of her own oldest son.

Marcia's mother was not close to her own mother, and seeing this recorded on the page made a strong impact on Marcia. Mother had not been mothered—she was forever on the outside of her mother's triangle, jealous of her sister's privileged position as Mother's favourite. This deprivation caused Marcia's mother much pain and despair.

Marcia knew it was her job to mother her mother. In her own words:

I remember a scene from my childhood, when I was very small and my mother was very ill. In fact she was suffering from acute depression. Nobody told me at the time, but nobody needs to tell me that now. She lay motionless in her bed in a darkened room which she had just decorated in shades of purple, with candles grouped around her bed table. The only sign of life was the lit end of her cigarette moving to her lips from time to time. This went on for days.

I felt angry and jealous that she got all the attention from my father when she was acting like such a wimp. If I did that, my brothers would have called me a baby and made my life hell!

At the same time, I felt her indescribable pain. Indescribable, and for me, completely incomprehensible.

Later, after Marcia had left home and established her own life style, she writes:

While my mother's direct attempts to control my behaviour had ceased, her dependency—her habit of wanting me to mediate between her and the world—grew very strong. I didn't even recognize it for ages—not until it became unbearable for me in my late 20s. I was taking care not only of Mom, but all of my clients, my son, my ex-husband, my current husband, both husbands' families, and anyone else who came along looking like they needed someone.

While I was pregnant with my second child, my mother had open-heart surgery. While in the intensive care unit, she had a psychotic attack. I saw real madness face to face, staring back at me, and I realized I could never, never fill that hole!

During that time I had a dream:

Mom was running toward the house where my father lives now. I was chasing her, begging her to stop making herself suffer. She was very small and weak. I picked her up and saw that she was getting smaller and weaker, and was going to die. I frantically ran to my father's house and begged for help. The people there just laughed. I was running into the hospital, carrying her in my arms, desperate, when I woke up.

That was a little over a year ago. Since then, with a woman guide/ therapist, I am learning to look at life in new ways—to hear and see both my internal and external worlds, past and present. I have learned to say "no." I have learned to listen to my heart. I have learned to allow those bad, irrational feelings which imprisoned my family so many years ago.

The more we focus on our own reality—what we hear, see, feel and want—the more we no longer see the world through our parents' eyes. This is saying goodbye to them as parents, and hello to them as people. In Marcia's case, it's saying goodbye to her role of mothering a mother who was never mothered, and beginning to mother herself. Questions to keep her focused might be: Do I save Mother or myself? Is it my life or hers?

Marcia concludes her story:

I know now that I can't help anyone by neglecting myself. I can't reach into my mother's head, heart, or life, and make it better.

Once, recently, for a brief moment, I caught myself just being with my mother with no guilt, no resentment, no anger, no pity, no fear. She was playing with my little son, her grandson. They had a little pillow and Mom would say "good night" and the baby would put his head down beside hers. Then they would both pop up and Mom would say "Good morning!" We all laughed hilariously. I felt connected to the world through this simple experience—the three of us coming together and laughing. I was seeing not my mother, but an old woman playing with a little boy.

I knew I was on the right track.

GUIDELINES

Preparing to Draw a Family Map and Genogram
- Visit childhood haunts to stir up memories.
- Ask questions of relatives.
- Identify family rules. Were they different for males and females? With older and younger members?
- Identify family roles.
- Search out family secrets.
- Perhaps include the following information:
    Professions
    Health
    Marital
    Children
    Ages and reason for death

Drawing a Family Map
Think of your family before you were 12 years old.
- Draw circles for your mother, father and yourself.
- Now add any brothers and sisters.
- Write names and present ages in circles.
- Draw lines according to legend from each person to every other person to indicate the kinds of relationships they have.
- Write an adjective or two to describe the role each person plays in the family (e.g., the star, the black sheep, the clown, the caretaker, etc.)

If you want to extend this research:
- Use coloured pens to indicate triangles in the system:
    The three most powerful people
    The three least powerful people
    The female triangle (if there is one)
    The male triangle (if there is one)
    If appropriate: Mom's kids, Dad's kids, the *good guys*, the *bad guys*

DRAWING A GENOGRAM. (USE DIAGRAM 6 TO GET STARTED.)
Gather information as in *Preparing to Draw*, then add:
- Each family member's profession.
- The families of grandmothers and grandfathers.
- Another generation if you like.
- Draw lines (according to the legend provided) to indicate the nature of an individual's relationship to the others, *where you think it's important.*
- Find the gender and generational themes.
- If this family had a book or song title, what would it be?

WRITING
- Learn family stories and write your own herstory.
- Write your life story as though it were a fairy tale.

HIGHLIGHTS

- Getting to know our roots might include:
  Visiting childhood haunts to stir up memories.
  Asking questions, especially about family secrets.
  Identifying family roles.

- Constructing a genogram and family map is an illuminating experience that may explain patterns in the daughter mother relationship. Family information is useful in defusing strong emotions in relationships.

- Use Diagram 6 on the following page to begin your own family genogram.

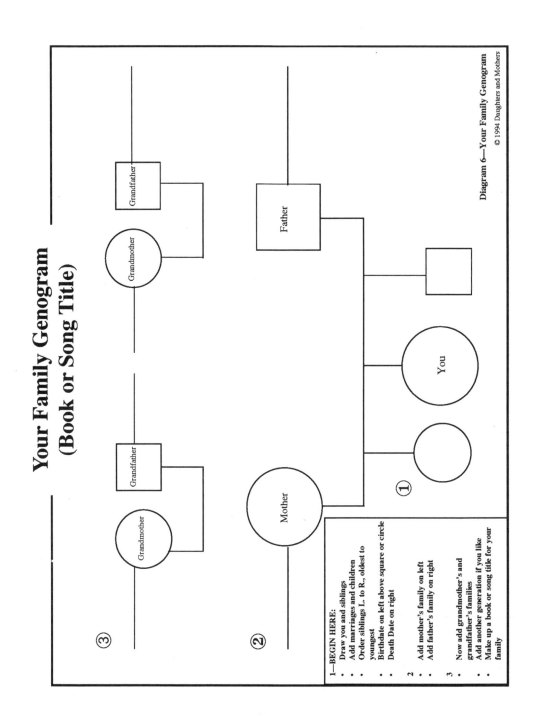

Your Family Genogram
(Book or Song Title)

Grandfather

Grandmother

Grandfather

Grandmother

Father

Mother

You

①

②
③

1—BEGIN HERE:
- Draw you and siblings
- Add marriages and children
- Order siblings L. to R., oldest to youngest
- Birthdate on left above square or circle
- Death Date on right

2
- Add mother's family on left
- Add father's family on right

3
- Now add grandmother's and grandfather's families
- Add another generation if you like
- Make up a book or song title for your family

Diagram 6—Your Family Genogram

© 1994 Daughters and Mothers

CHAPTER 3

Persephone descended into the underworld to recover lost parts of herself through knowing her mother's people, the Demetreioi.

3

GETTING
TO KNOW
OUR MOTHER

Researching Mother's childhood can begin with looking at family pictures and visiting with relatives who knew her. Mother is a human being, a woman who, like you, was shaped by her experiences as a daughter.

If we come from a disengaged relationship with Mother, getting to know more about her provides a needed connection. If we come from an enmeshed relationship, the search provides needed separation. Knowing her history allows us to release Mother from a narrow one-dimensional box and Daughter from a distorted heritage.

JACKIE'S STORY
Three women—Grandmother Mary, Mother Lillian and Daughter Jackie are portrayed here—three generations of women as seen through Jackie's eyes. During the past months, Jackie has consulted with a therapist to help her deal with memories of her mother who recently died. Jackie's impressions of her hypercritical mother, Lillian, were vivid.

> *I was never good enough; my work or my appearance always needed straightening. Lillian was a demanding, over-critical, domineering mother. She played the role of perfect wife and hostess; my role was to make her look like the perfect mother.*

For months, Jackie's anger and hurt feelings came tumbling out. Her therapist listened and supported Jackie's anguish. When the intensity of her pain diminished, she asked, "Who mothered Mother? What do you know about your grand-mother?"

Why should I find out? I didn't like my mother and I don't want to know about her childhood.

Still, the therapist's questions about her grandmother, Mary, aroused Jackie's curiosity about her mother's growing-up years. She found many blanks in the family history. "I feel guilty asking questions about my mother, now that she is dead. Should I not leave well enough alone?" she asked anxiously. With her therapist's encouragement Jackie began looking through old photo albums and taping stories of Lillian's youth.

In the mildewed family album Jackie found several photo-graphs of Lillian with her brothers and sister. One of these caught her attention—Lillian, wearing a starched middy blouse, shy and unsmiling, posed in front of the farm house with her sister. A poem was scrawled on the back of the photo:

> *There was a little girl who had a little curl*
> *Right in the middle of her forehead.*
> *When she was good, she was very very good —*
> *But when she was bad, she was horrid.*

To Jackie, the poem showed a more rebellious side of the "nice" little girl her mother appeared to be in the photo. Spurred on to learn more, Jackie made a trip to her cousin's house where she heard many interesting and amusing stories about her mother's childhood. The cousin told this story.

Your mother was called Lil for short, and being the youngest daughter, she received special treatment. She always managed to disappear just when the garden needed weeding, the pastry rolled out, or the Sunlight soap slivered into small pieces for the washing machine. Reading Eaton's Catalogue in the outhouse, she pretended not to hear Mother's voice calling her to do the chores.

Lil was raised in a small farm community soon after the turn of the century. When the winter roads became impassable she boarded in town with her aunt and uncle so she could attend school. Even though she was still under the thumb of her relatives, the arrangement afforded some freedom from her parents. No young woman of the time was allowed to leave home except to get married, but living with close relatives satisfied the demands of society.

During the summer, her parents chaperoned her carefully. Although public dance halls were strictly forbidden, Lillian and her younger brother would sneak out to go dancing. Do you know, they were never caught! In her 20s, she formally entertained her friends at her aunt's house, holding her own "at home soirées". I was shooed out of the room and forbidden to mention these flirtatious activities to Lillian's suitor, a young man from out of town who courted her on weekends, and later became her husband.

Jackie was moved by these stories of her mother as a girl. She had only seen the stern perfectionist wife and mother, not the fun-loving, daring woman. Here was a young woman who could sneak out to dances and keep a secret from her parents— very different from Jackie's earlier view of a prudish, critical woman. Both were parts of the same person. Jackie wished her mother had shared her memories before she died. If she had, Jackie might not have felt driven to be the perfect daughter.

A reunion with a girlhood friend reminded Jackie of a wonderful summer memory about her mother as a playful person.

My friend and I spent many summers at a hotel resort with our families. As little girls, when we had been sent upstairs to bed, we would peek over the banister and watch the entertainment in the hotel lobby. Our fathers had stayed in the city working, and now we saw our mothers cutting loose. They had assembled all the guests for a demonstration of their special powers—ESP and hypnotism, no less! Unknown to the guests, they had a secret code. Their act was quite impressive to the guests—and us kids. "That's my mother, star of the show!" I thought.

Why had Jackie "forgotten" that memory of her mother as an entertainer? Most people don't take kindly to their parents trying on new and unusual behaviours. Somehow, we forget those incidents that are incompatible with the need to see Mother in a certain way. Adult children censor their own memories to protect the idealized view of their mother. The stereotype remains until the daughter is ready to stop and take stock of her life. This process led Jackie to see her mother as a person in her own right.

Jackie carried the research back another generation to Grandmother Mary. She sought out her cousin again, this time asking, "Who mothered Mother?" The cousin responded:

During the late 1800s, women had their babies at home under the experienced care of midwives and female relatives. Grandmother Mary was the pillar of the community. She took pride in being the first visitor when any of her kin gave birth. To each farmhouse she brought gifts of hand-crocheted baby's woolens, homemade preserves, baked goods and advice. Her stern advice was not so readily welcomed. She would order the newly-delivered mother to get up and return to her duties. "Hoeing potatoes after a baby never did me any harm," she'd tell them.

This same woman could be very gentle with a crying baby, crooning lullabies while rocking it to sleep. She was loving and generous, yet stern and unyielding when it came to her high standards. Grandmother Mary silenced the tears of her own

children with the words, "I'll give you something to cry about!"
While she thought she was solving a problem, such a harsh
attitude only compounded the child's pain. Mary's children, upon
hearing those threatening words, became fast learners: "If you
knew what was good for you, you'd shut up real quick. You'd
swallow those tears and the big lump in your throat and get better
real fast!"

Jackie repeated these stories about Grandmother Mary to her therapist. "You know, this all seems very familiar to me. My feelings were not allowed, and tears were a nuisance. My mother used to say to me, 'Don't be so silly—stop being so silly.' I don't believe my mother could handle her children's feelings. Nor could her mother. How sad! My mother inherited her mother's world and I inherited hers. The buck must stop here! I want to help my children understand the traits of generosity, leadership and domination that were passed down through the female line."

Fortunately for Jackie, her father was more open about feelings. He legitimized her emotions by saying "You've got a wonderful temper, and I hope you never lose it," and "You look upset. Tell Daddy what's wrong."

Jackie recalled how her mother coped after her father died. They had been married 45 years.

Mom mourned privately and, in time, regained her sense of
independence, adventure and joy. Even after suffering a heart
attack, poor memory and failing health, she lived a productive 20
years as a widow.

Jackie was sorry she had never known the more daring side of her mother. Lillian broke family rules, tried new behaviours, and developed her own values. She struggled to become a person distinct from her family while still remaining attached. Although her adolescence seemed exciting, with the events of marriage and childbirth she abandoned this search for her own identity and followed the family traditions. Being female in this conservative family meant being overly responsible, extremely capable, and stern with her children. She never hinted that she had a different side in her youth.

Jackie compared her value system to Lillian's. Values she learned from her mother were: knowing one's place and doing one's duty. Although the words may never have been said, Lillian knew instinctively that she, not her husband, was in charge of making the marriage work. She raised the children, was responsible for their outcome, not asking her husband to be an equal parent. Jackie felt this same sombre seriousness about life, but tempered her views about real partnership in a marriage. She held herself and her husband equally accountable for developing a healthy family and marriage. Making the shift from over-responsibility for others to self-responsibility changed these old generational patterns.

As she continued her deliberations around her mother's and grandmother's history, more similarities began to emerge. Both women had been wily and fun-loving when they were young, but serious-minded, overly competent and stern as wives and mothers. After the children were raised, they were once again lighthearted, sexual and playful. Jackie noted this was true of her own life as well.

Jackie confronted the myth that held women to be caregivers exclusively, sacrificing self-development for the care and nurture of families and husbands. From Mary's generation down to the present, this strongly-held belief has lessened in intensity. In Mary's day, a mother was not supposed to have a life of her own, a room of her own, time of her own, except perhaps a hobby to keep her "out of trouble."

What happens when women neglect their own aspirations and gifts? In her research, Jackie saw how frustration is often followed by depressive, domineering and obsessive behaviour.

Mary's domineering turned into Lillian's criticism which became Jackie's bossiness.

As a result of her work, Jackie realized that to a large extent Mary and Lillian had fewer choices available to them. They made the best of their lives. Today Jackie has more options and makes more conscious choices. She shifts the legacy passed down from her ancestors by curbing her bossiness. She welcomes the inherited gifts of generosity, passion, and creativity. Gaining a multidimensional picture of her mother helps her to create a different future.

GUIDELINES

Researching

- Select a relative or friend who might shed some light on your mother's childhood.

- Arrange to visit this person.

- Tape your conversation or make notes in your journal.

- Take along some questions and family photos to "prime the pump."

- Go back to the neighbourhood where your mother was raised.

- Take snapshots of her childhood home, school, synagogue or church, a favourite playground or corner store if they still exist.

- Ask yourself the following questions and record your answers in a journal.

    —What is the worst thing you could find out about your mother?

    —The worst thing she could find out about you?

    —What is the best thing you could find out?

    —The best thing she could discover about you?

- What were the significant events in your mother's growing up years?

    —In her adult years?

    —How did these events shape her?

    —How do they affect you?

- What were the family secrets? If you don't know, ask or guess.

- If Mother is available, ask her what she felt about her childhood. If she is unavailable, use your intuition. Compare this information with your own childhood feelings.

Drawing

In Chapter 2, you may have done your own family map. Now make one for Mother's family.

- Take a blank piece of paper.

- Draw three circles—one for your mother, one your maternal grandmother, and one for grandfather. Add names, present ages or ages at death.

- Draw lines to connect the circles (see Chapter 2).

- Add Mother's brothers and sisters.

- Write three adjectives to describe each of them.

- What were their occupations, health, marital status, and roles.

- Let this map speak to you.

- Describe what you think it was like for your mother to grow up female.

- Take your family map drawing from Chapter 2 and place it beside Mother's map.

- What are some similar patterns? Which are different?

HIGHLIGHTS

- Getting to know Mother as a young girl creates equality in the relationship. Mother's family history affects how she mothered you and how you mother your children.

- Knowing how others experienced your mother as a child and young woman humanizes her.

- You can choose which of Mother's values to affirm and which to discard.

- In doing this research, there are four stages to explore which are interchangeable and may not occur in any specific sequence.

Four Stages of Family Research:

1. **Feelings**—We need to express the complex feelings about Mother. See Chapter 5.

2. **Research Jitters**—Expect resistance. It may take the form of reluctance, anxiety, denial, procrastination or fear of what may be uncovered.

3. **The Research Project**—Choose a plan that is manageable and a cheerleader to encourage you.

4. **Understanding and Integrating Mother's History**— can facilitate acceptance of ourselves.

CHAPTER 4

We can speculate that Demeter and Persephone had a warm and involved relationship. As the women evolved, the relationship grew into an interdependent one. When Persephone broke the news she intended to work with souls in the under-world, both had to acknowledge their different responsibilities. From that moment on, each goddess had to follow her own intuition.

4

GETTING TO KNOW OUR RELATIONSHIP WITH MOTHER

This chapter introduces Five Different Types of Relationship Styles between daughters and mothers. Each relationship style is placed on a *continuum*—a sliding scale from one extreme to another. Some of us flow between styles, others remain fixed. Each style carries a short description which may or may not sound familiar. Five daughters tell their stories that illustrate these styles, followed by suggestions for change.

Since relationships are complex and interwoven, a chart helps give us a handle on our past relationships, how this keeps us stuck today, and what we can do now.

The chart is meant simply to describe, not blame. (See Diagram 7.)

We can use it as a guideline to discover our own patterns of relating. Nobody fits one style alone. Most of us overlap two or more relationship modes. We may even shift from one to another over a period of time.

Look over the Five Relationship Styles on Diagram 7.

Five Relationship Styles
for Daughters and Mothers

Best Buddies	Never the Twain Shall meet	Friends	Nothing in Common	Strangers
Overconnected	Overconnected	Healthy connection	Lack of connection	Isolated, disconnected
Enmeshed: too close	Enmeshed: conflicted	Engaged, flexible	Disengaged, out of touch	Disengaged, emotionally cut off
Can't disagree	Can't agree; confrontive	Can both agree and disagree	Seldom see each other	Hardly speak for years
Too cheerful or too grim	Too angry; denies love	Can express many feelings	Sad, depressed feelings; conscious or repressed	Angry or hateful; conscious or repressed
Too dependent	Independent	Interdependent	Ambivalent about being dependent/independent	Independent
Daughter mothers Mother; Mother expects to be like her daughter	Mother is critical, perhaps abusive	Cares for self and others	Daughter may have mothered Mother; longs for closeness	Little or no mothering for either
Denies differences	Denies similarities	Aware of differences and similarities	Unaware of differences and similarities	Denies similarities
Fears rejection	Fears engulfment	Understands and accepts	Fears abandonment	Fears intimacy

Diagram 7
Relationship Styles

RELATIONSHIP #1:
Best Buddies

- Overconnected

- Enmeshed: too close

- Cannot disagree

- Too cheerful or too grim

- Too Dependent

- Daughter mothers Mother; Mother forces her identity on Daughter

- Denies differences

- Fears rejection

Whether Daughter lives under the same roof or moves halfway across the world, she and Mother may still be overinvolved. To determine the degree of enmeshment, look at whether Daughter has developed her own life independent of her mother. If she is arrested in her growth, perhaps she has not moved through the necessary developmental stages of building a career, becoming financially independent, and creating her own community.

Caroline's Story

The snapshot in Caroline's hand could be entitled "The family that prays together stays together." The family is standing stiffly in front of their farm home, wearing their Sunday winter coats. Judging by their flat expressions, neither Mother, Caroline nor her brother want their pictures taken, but are posing to please Dad. This first generation Canadian family looks cautious and controlled.

Caroline returns the snapshot to the album. When Dad died five years ago, her younger brother moved to the city. Now there were just the two of them, 33-year-old Caroline and her 65-year-old Mother.

She ruminates, "Why did I feel so disloyal looking for apartments this afternoon? I have everything I need right here at home. Surely there must be exceptions to the rule that young people have to move out on their own? Moving out seems so difficult and ridiculous. Someday this will be mine anyway. I wish Dad were here to tell me what to do."

When her father died, Caroline assumed his role of caring for Mother. She is aging rapidly and needs help with chores like shovelling the walk and buying groceries. She also wants someone to remind her to take her insulin and keep her company.

Caroline agrees with her mother's disparaging remarks about the neighbours, thereby distancing themselves from the community. Since her brother's things are stored in the spare bedroom, Caroline sleeps in her mother's bedroom. She acquiesces to her mother's decision that the third bedroom is nice as a TV den. Vaguely she wonders why her brother doesn't move his things out. He was always treated as the golden boy. Sometimes she fantasizes about having a room of her own.

For this pair, the world is a dangerous place. They need each other as a security blanket to ward off anxiety. The pattern of overenmeshment is a family system that probably developed over several generations. Caroline can only break this pattern with outside help that is stronger than the family.

Daughter's Work: Becoming independent.

- Finding a supportive friend or counselor.
- Reclaiming your identity and personal power.
- Identifying the differences between you and your mother.

- Focusing on your interests and needs.

- Listing life goals and beginning to develop them.

- Separating gradually from Mother.

- Connecting with siblings and friends in the community.

- Moving out of the house or creating a separate apartment at home.

- Moving from dependence to independence.

- Taking charge of your life.

- Using your energy to be proactive for yourself rather than reactive to Mother.

RELATIONSHIP #2:
Never the Twain Shall Meet

- Overconnected

- Enmeshed: conflicted

- Can't agree; confrontive

- Too angry; denies love

- Independent

- Mother is critical, perhaps abusive

- Denies similarities

- Fears engulfment

The connecting bond in this relationship is criticism and judgement. Mother learned to argue growing up in her family. For her, disagreement is a substitute for intimacy. Daughter resists claiming her identity except through reacting to her mother. Daughter wavers between angry and hurt feelings while repressing loving feelings.

Lisa's Story

When she hears knocking at the door, Lisa dashes down from the upstairs nursery where the baby has just fallen asleep.

"What kept you?" her mother snaps. "Where were you? Sleeping all day? My it's dark in here. I'll just open some curtains. Here are some groceries we picked up on our way into town. We don't mind where we sleep as long as the mattress is firm. Your father has a sore back." Her mother pushes past Lisa and walks into the small living room.

Lisa's parents, who live 100 miles away, have arrived unannounced, as is the custom in her family. Her mother continues: "Your father is here for some tests and we won't get in your way. My, your house seems dark; it must be the dark paint. Either that or the windows are dirty."

Lisa interrupts, "It took me a month to recover from your last visit, and you still haven't said you're sorry for our fight. Dad, you stay out of this. Don't take your coats off. I can't put you up. I'll make a reservation for you at the hotel. Why didn't you phone first? I hate being disturbed while the baby and I nap!" The confrontation continues, as usual.

Lisa has gone through periods when she said nothing in reply to her mother's criticisms but simmered inside, later complaining to her best friend or her husband. She continues to blame her mother for the negativity between them, instead of taking responsibility for changing the relationship.

Daughter's Work: Becoming independent

- Devising a plan of action to stop the conflict.
- Stop reacting and be proactive.
- Separating while remaining connected.

- Researching ways to be positive.

- Being heard and supported by someone other than Mother.

- Choosing short, specific occasions to limit time together.

- Discovering one way Mother can help: make a casserole, babysit, fix the plumbing, paint a room, mow the lawn.

- Telling Mother she has 15 minutes to be as critical as she wants and then criticism will be unacceptable for the remainder of the visit.

- Setting boundaries: phoning before coming to visit; defining length of stay; determining acceptable topics of conversation.

RELATIONSHIP #3:
Friends

- Healthy connection

- Engaged, flexible

- Can both agree and disagree

- Can express many feelings

- Interdependent

- Cares for self and others

- Aware of differences and similarities

- Understands and accepts

Both Mother and Daughter have a strong sense of identity. They enjoy both living apart and being together. Theirs is a healthy relationship where each takes responsibility for herself. They acknowledge both their differences and their similarities. They can argue over differences yet remain friends. They can express their feelings and trust each other.

Having Fun Together

A mother and daughter are baking a birthday cake for their friend. The recipe card has become so soiled it is almost unreadable. Following directions as far as they can, they wind up with a batter that is like cement. They begin to improvise, adding first a dozen eggs, then a pint of cream, finally a bottle of kahlua. The mixer spins out the concoction in all directions, spattering the dough all over the kitchen and the cooks. The two women dissolve into fits of laughter at how ridiculous they are.

This mother and daughter love and respect each other. They both agree and disagree, accepting each other's strengths and differences. They live separate and satisfying lives. Sometimes they attend movies together, share an occasional shopping trip or dine out. Interdependent and connected, each is self-supporting with her own residence. Each pursues career interests and creates her own circle of friends and nurturing relationships in her community.

Daughter's Work: Becoming Interdependent

- Separating geographically from Mother and becoming your own person—moving out and forward into your own life.

- Engaging Mother on points of disagreement and agreement.

- Stating differences and similarities.

- Managing conflict creatively.

- Standing your own ground and controlling your life.

- Deliberately choosing times to be close to Mother.
- Creating your own life and circle of friends

RELATIONSHIP #4:
NOTHING IN COMMON

- Lack of connection
- Disengaged, out of touch
- Seldom see each other
- Sad, depressed feelings; conscious or repressed
- Ambivalent about being dependent or independent
- Daughter may have mothered Mother; longs for closeness
- Unaware of differences and similarities
- Fears abandonment

CYNTHIA'S STORY

Cynthia reads her mother's letter aloud to her therapist. "'Old Joe died of cancer last week and Rita Black committed suicide. I handle life by going with adversity, adjusting and accepting and then ignoring it. I try not to think about it and keep busy. Rita was living on her own—sounds like she was feeling down for years.' The whole letter goes like that," grimaces Cynthia, "ignoring me and not mentioning her feelings towards me."

Cynthia hasn't been to see her mother since Christmas and now it is spring. They write sporadically to each other. Cynthia, a social worker in a city hospital, feels little connection to her widowed mother living in her rural home town.

Cynthia's therapist asks how she feels while reading the letter.

"I don't feel anything," admits Cynthia. "She doesn't mean much to me and doesn't want to understand me. I just feel blank." After a few moments of silence Cynthia adds, "I guess I feel sad."

The therapist directs Cynthia back to the letter. "Read between the lines and see what your mother is trying to say."

After a long pause, Cynthia asks "Could she be trying to tell me that she gets depressed too? I wonder if she's worried about cancer, or about dying alone. Maybe she even worries about me living alone in the big city."

Cynthia was about to dismiss her mother's letter as inconsequential and having nothing to do with her . The habit of being disconnected was so ingrained that it took an outsider to reconnect Cynthia with her mother. Mother too feels distanced, and doesn't know how to bridge the gap. Both may be aware of their longing for closeness, but are unable to reach out. They need help interpreting one to the other.

Daughter's Work: Facing the fear of dependency and abandonment

- Developing a connection with Mother.
- Opening to compassion and positive feelings.
- Understanding how we continue to deaden ourselves and the relationship.
- Asking Mother questions about childhood—ours and hers.
- Discovering what happened during both mother's early life and ours that might cause the lack of connection.
- Exploring ways of being together: take a walk, share family snapshots, read aloud to each other.

RELATIONSHIP #5:
STRANGERS

- Disconnected

- Disengaged, emotionally cut-off

- Hardly speak for years

- Angry or hateful; conscious or repressed

- Independent and isolated

- Little or no mothering for either

- Denies similarities

- Fears intimacy

Long-forgotten traumatic events from childhood can account for the complete emotional cutoff experienced by adult daughters. The trauma may be long forgotten, caused by the death of a parent, a family crisis, incest, or a natural disaster such as fire or flood. Whatever happened, positive feelings about each other have been buried. This results in emotional deprivation for both mother and daughter.

There is no answer to the question of why some babies manage miraculously to survive and adapt in spite of deprived mothering. Perhaps they come into the world with stronger spirits than others. The mother or caregiver cannot bond with her baby for reasons beyond her control, probably related to her own background. She goes through the motions but her heart is closed. The baby senses her despair and closes her heart as well, learning not to demand anything from her mother. If the mother sees no demands, she makes no responses. She withdraws further and continues a vicious circle.

Darlene's Story

The phone rings and Darlene cringes. As Christmas time approaches, she hates to answer the phone: it might be her mother calling from New Zealand with her cheerful Christmas message.

Darlene resents her mother's intrusions into the life she has made for herself in Canada. She left home as a teenager, never to return. She has nothing in common with her overseas relatives. Nothing! Her mother was too busy to pay attention to her when she was growing up, so Darlene feels no connection with her now. She feels only resentment.

Darlene has many reasons for her anger and sees no need to respond to the duty telephone call once a year. Still, she is surprised to feel such intense hate.

Finally the phone stops ringing. Next time Darlene knows she will answer it, and find herself grimacing as she replies in monosyllables to her mother's polite inquiries. She will then resist any connection for yet another year.

Daughter's Work: Facing the fear of intimacy and dependency

- Using therapy to help make a limited connection.
- Finding someone to hear and support us when we experience grief and rage.
- Remembering and understanding traumatic events through therapy and journalling.
- Developing respect and some positive feelings for Mother.
- Understanding that deprived mothering caused the disconnection between us and Mother.
- Initiating some small reconciliation with Mother on our terms, i.e. exchange letters and cards on special occasions.

GUIDELINES

Reflecting

These questions are guidelines for thinking about your relationship. If you like, write out your answers, or simply spend some time remembering and reflecting. Recall details and examples.

1. a) In what ways are you similar to your mother?

    b) In what ways are you different from your mother?

2. a) What do you value most about yourself as a person?

    b) What do you value most about your mother?

3. List some of the values, attitudes and behaviours that you have learned from your mother.

4. Discover where you fit on the Daughter/Mother Relationship Continuum. When you determine your relationship style, consider the various guidelines offered. Only you can decide where to begin your work.

5. List some of the values, attitudes and behaviours learned from your mother that you have chosen to discard.

6. a) Think of an experience with your mother when you felt misunderstood.

    b) Think of an experience with your mother when you felt understood.

7. What are five small steps you are ready to take in the near future to change your relationship?

HIGHLIGHTS

This chapter describes five relationship styles, each with a range of behaviours (See Diagram 7).

1. Best Buddies—Enmeshed, too close

2. Never the Twain Shall Meet—Enmeshed, conflicted

3. Friends—Engaged, flexible

4. Nothing in common—Disengaged, out of touch

5. Strangers—Disengaged, emotionally cut off

CHAPTER 5

When Persephone left her mother, she felt excitement at beginning her life work. Then she felt fear as she descended into the unknown. In the darkness she felt the pain of her innermost emotions as she embraced the souls of the dead. Demeter's reaction was dismay at her daughter's choice. Then she went into deep mourning as she wandered the earth, unable to rest, unable to work. When at last Persephone ascended to the upper world, both mother and daughter cried and laughed, hugged and danced.

5

GETTING
TO KNOW
OUR FEELINGS

Feelings are invaluable tools in separating from Mother and in reconnecting in new ways. Persephone and Demeter ran the gamut of feelings as they separated and were transformed.

Repressed feelings can contaminate our health and block our growth. By expressing them, we bring ourselves out of the deadness of repression back into the stream of life. Releasing feelings releases the energy that we used to repress them. By itself, energy is good, the gift of life. How we use it can be either good or bad according to our intentions.

Emotions are going on inside us every moment of every day. We just have to tune in to them. They are a unique expression of our deeper selves. Bringing us closer to others, feelings provide the connection for which we long.

The most grievous loss in life is the loss of our feelings. If these were not affirmed by our parents when we were children, we learn to deny them. Paradoxically, when we control them through denial, they end up controlling us. It is only by acknowledging and expressing them that the energy they contain is available.

Grief is one of life's crises that call forth emotions long suppressed. Experiencing the loss of a child, mate, parent, job or dream will put this process into motion. Intense feelings of anger and sadness, as well as sleeplessness, restlessness, irritability and general depression are symptoms of grief.

A present day crisis also triggers unfinished work with our parents: things not said, not confronted, not felt, not shared. This is the time daughters are most likely to examine their relationship with Mother.

As women we may define ourselves solely by the roles we play. If we haven't examined these roles, we are prisoners of our childhood families. If left to operate unconsciously, the unexamined messages and behaviours we absorb about being female, about being a mother or daughter, about relationships, relentlessly pursue and control us, like a tail wagging a dog. Unacknowledged, these important messages remain unavailable for examination, renegotiation and change.

This chapter explores Three Stages in getting to know our feelings: *acknowledgement, expression* and *integration*.

ACKNOWLEDGEMENT

We are afraid of being overwhelmed by our feelings, whether they are pain, fear, anger, or love, because we believe they are potentially dangerous. If they go unacknowledged, they can escalate. By exploring our feelings in a safe place, we gain confidence in our ability to use them wisely.

As these emotions build in strength, we may feel out of control and start to question ourselves. These unnamed feelings can become so persistent that we are finally forced to recognize their existence.

MARCIA'S STORY CONTINUES
When I was a child, I watched my mother experiencing a lot of very

intense feelings about herself, her life, her situation as a housewife and mother. Very unhappy feelings! Our people are very WASP, and these emotions were perceived as irrational and therefore bad. Feelings were not acknowledged as real or reasonable. When intense, they must be kept in their place and endured privately until they pass.

I helped protect my mother from these terrible feelings by placating, making everyone laugh, and doing extra chores. I was crucified between my need to be a good daughter in continuing to protect and help my mother, and my terrible grief at the certainty that it was a completely impossible task.

Most of us dislike dredging up the despair of yesterday. However, this is a necessary part of healing. When feelings are released in an accepted environment, strength and self-acceptance follow. From this process come peace and forgiveness.

Jackie's Story Continues

After the death of her father, anxiety attacks flooded through the cracks of this competent, well-defended woman. Jackie disregarded the nagging agitation and the depressive fogs that enveloped her several times a month. When her anxiety threatened to overwhelm her, she phoned a therapist. She wanted a quick cure to banish her panic so she could get on with her well-ordered life.

In her first session she explained, "Everything was fine in my life. Suddenly I've got the shakes. I'm afraid all the time. Am I going crazy?"

Jackie didn't want to admit that something was out of balance in her life. But her anxiety and depression forced her to take herself seriously for the first time. It was the discomfort she wanted quickly fixed that led her to reach out for healing. Once she took that step, she was on the way to discovering herself.

EXPRESSION

Too many of us spend our lives unconsciously re-enacting old scenarios, engendering negative feelings in ourselves and instilling this process in our children. Since feelings are powerful clues to our identity, expressing them can help us to act consciously and responsibly.

As babies we come into the world fully expressive. All our feelings are intense. Usually, though not always, Mother is our first mirror. Our first impulses are directed at our primary caregiver. If her emotional range is curtailed, the baby's expressiveness is also limited.

Within the home we quickly learn that acceptable feelings can be expressed directly, while the rest are shamed into silence. Some families allow only cheerful countenances, while others reject any emotions at all.

As adults we are intimidated by the parents we still carry inside us. This blocks us from re-experiencing forbidden feelings. However, memories usually cannot be suppressed forever. When they begin surfacing, we have the opportunity to express the emotions engendered by these memories in order to heal ourselves.

Fiona's Story

Fiona, an educator and administrator, sits stiffly, jaw clenched, lips pursed. In her childhood family, males could explode with anger while females were allowed only tears and sarcasm.

Fiona speaks in a monotone, her clenched fists the only sign of her buried rage. "I'm 55 years old," she says. "Mom and Dad are both dead, but I still try to be nice to everyone. I hate it!"

As Fiona owns her anger in therapy, she is encouraged to hit a pillow or the well-padded arm of the chair as she talks. Her clenched fist is her guide. "It's safe to give your fist a voice in here," her therapists says encouragingly. "Yell out all the things you've never yelled."

With much prompting, Fiona finds her voice as well as her fist and begins her work. Afterwards, jaws and fists released, with a sparkle in her face, she comments, "That feels good!"

"You are good," the therapist replies.

JACKIE'S STORY CONTINUES

As therapy proceeded, Jackie's blank face began to show her fear. Her voice changed from a dull monotone to choked sobs. At home and in therapy she continued to express her fears. Then one evening in a women's group, she began shaking and weeping uncontrollably. Her friends held her, providing a strong container for the force of her feelings until they subsided.

Jackie learned not only to endure, but also to enjoy the energy from her feelings. She began to take better care of herself, eat better, get massages, keep a journal, spend time with friends, and relax to soothing music.

INTEGRATION

When we act self-responsibly rather than unconsciously, we are integrating the disowned parts of ourselves. When we act on behalf of ourselves rather than acting out feelings, we have begun to own our behaviour, beliefs and feelings.

Taking time to reflect on our feelings and beliefs is an integrative process.

JOAN'S STORY CONTINUES

Joan is a woman who mothered Mother and was not mothered herself. Doubled up with pain, she blurts out her anguish in a therapy session.

I wish my mother was dead. It is easier to wish her dead than to feel this pain. It's easier to wish her dead than to have to change.

I now believe she was developmentally arrested at 9 years old. This helps me to give up wanting her to see me. She was never able to be a mother or a friend to me. It also helps me give up trying to make her 'grow up.'"

After much work, the tone of Joan's voice changes:

With some success, I am going through a much-needed separation from Mother. I am pleased that I no longer jump in to save her. I feel calm more often. Maybe the pain is for life, just as my tubal ligation is for life, but it is bearable now.

Joan's work has brought some rewards. She no longer needs medication to be able to sleep at night. She feels more pleasure and comfort within herself.

MARCIA'S STORY CONTINUES

Marcia has worked through her feelings with her mother and has reached some resolution.

For years I had nothing but anger for my mother. Then, after months of painfully sifting through my psyche the dam broke. Dropping my mother off one evening, I waited, as usual, to make sure she got into her building safely. As I watched her walk away from the car, I was suddenly shaken by a vision of her as a young woman—a woman about my age, the age she would have been when I was a small child. It was as if a film image of the tall, graceful young woman with dark hair and fashionable clothes was overlaid on top of the arthritic old woman she had become.

The vision pierced me right through. First, I felt rage: rage that she was not my mother any more; instead, she had abandoned me to become an old woman who herself needed mothering from me. Then the rage gave way to intense grief. As I drove home I was sobbing violently, uncontrollably, thinking over and over 'I want my real mother back.' After a time, enormous love and gratitude filled me. I remembered, all at once, how she had supported me and stuck up for me against my tormenting older brothers, how she looked after me when I was sick. As I felt remorse for the years of anger and bitterness, I wept with grief and love. I continued to weep as the memories surfaced and swept over me. Thank heaven for traffic. I sobbed for nearly an hour as I drove through the city and then parked behind my house.

For me the experience was a letting go. My emotional range with my mother had narrowed to a tight-lipped irritation which had remained for years. By finding—and then breaking through—the rage and grief I had forbidden myself to feel, I was able to re-discover the love and other feelings that were also part of the relationship. I knew intellectually that I had to let go of the image of my mother as Mother. I had to see that image of her as a young woman to activate the part of me that was really holding on—the angry, abandoned child who believed she must be bad because she had terrible, unreasonable feelings.

GUIDELINES

Writing

Sentence Completion—This exercise may help you expand your own repertoire of feelings. Complete the sentences:

> I feel sad when...
> I feel guilty when...
> I feel angry when...
> I feel pleasure when...
> I feel happy when...
> I can trust when...
> I feel pain when...

Reflecting

- Think back to your childhood. Recall what feelings were supported and what were discouraged in your family.
- What feelings were allowed?
- What feelings were not allowed?
- What feelings were owned by the females?
- Were they different from those owned by the males? How?
- What about grandmother and grandfather?
- What was the most pervasive feeling tone coming from your mother?
- What was the most pervasive feeling felt by you as a young daughter?
- What feelings are you allowed today?
- What feelings would you like to change?
- In planning for your future, what feelings would you like to feel?

FEELING

Let your body speak to you. Locate those sensations within your body.

- Find a quiet place, relax your body and close your eyes.

- Place your hands on your tummy. What are you feeling right now? A tightness, or soreness, or a flutter, perhaps? Where is it located?

- Place your hand on that spot. Stay close to the sensations as you breathe deeply.

- Let your body speak to you.

- Describe the sensation you are experiencing. What are you feeling? Is it close to mad, glad, scared, sad? Take ownership of this feeling, or these mixed feelings. It is yours!

- Express this feeling out loud—with your voice, with your body.

THE FEELINGS CIRCLE DIAGRAM

Sad, Mad, Glad Scared is a simple model to understand feelings. This circle is divided arbitrarily into four sections. It doesn't include all feelings. Since our emotions can be difficult to name, it helps to simplify them in this way. Within each section too, there are variations and degrees of intensity. Identify the feelings you have experienced and those you wish to experience more completely.

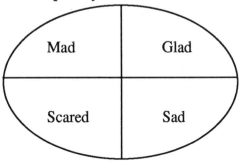

Unwrapping Mad

The emotion we sometimes call mad, like most emotions, is an illusive one, masking other deeper emotions.

- There are shades and differences within this one emotion.

- Some of us would not acknowledge *mad* as part of our repertoire, yet would acknowledge a milder feeling, like *annoyance, impatience, irritation*, depending on the context of the situation.

- If we were to unwrap the group of feelings called *mad* and spread it out on a continuum, it might look like this:

> Slightly mad——Moderately mad——Intensely mad

More Writing

- Look at the *Mad* scale.
- Pick out one feeling.
- Remember the situation when you last felt this feeling.
- Write out the scenario.
- Look to the next words on the scale. Are any of these familiar to you?
- Stretch your imagination to recall a scene where you felt more of these feelings.
- We can expand our range of feelings without necessarily acting them out., e.g., we can feel anger, acknowledge it and not act it out in harmful ways.
- Move on to explore the feelings *Glad, Sad, Scared* in the same way.

Slightly glad——Moderately glad——Intensely glad

Slightly sad——Moderately sad——Intensely sad

Slightly scared-Moderately scared—Intensely scared

Ambivalence or mixed feelings

Many of us experience two or more conflicting feelings at once. When we are ambivalent, it is difficult to sort it all out. Combinations of feelings may appear in most of the emotions: guilt, frustration, anger, confusion, shame, humiliation, joy, forgiveness, depression and fear.

- The next time you feel ambivalent or confused, write out the incident in detail.

- Turn to the Feelings Circle Diagram and see where you fit.

- Make a game plan. Express your feelings to yourself and a trusted other. What actions will you take? How will this information make a difference in your life? What choices will you make?

- You are more than your feelings, even though they are important.

- Let yourself feel good. Congratulate yourself on taking time to find out more about yourself.

HIGHLIGHTS

- Feelings are energy. Energy is powerful. We can use energy to replace inherited misery by recreating ourselves anew.

- A woman in mid-life who hasn't examined her many roles and feels dissatisfied with her life is a prisoner of social conditioning.

- Acknowledging, expressing and acting on our feelings are three different phases toward releasing them.

- Although discovering our feelings will lead us to recover lost parts of ourselves, we are not simply our feelings.

- We can talk about a feeling we have rather than act it out.

- To simplify the identification of feelings, try placing them within these categories: Sad, Mad, Glad, Scared.

- Ambivalence is experiencing two or more conflicting feelings at once.

- Being heard, supported and accepted by a trusted friend or therapist helps us accept who we are—the worst and the best. A therapist can help defuse intense, overwhelming feelings while validating their authenticity. There is hope in this work.

- Pain can be transformed into self-acceptance, strength, forgiveness, and peace.

CHAPTER 6

Persephone's childhood messages are not known. Making her journey into the underworld to learn about the positive and negative messages from her ancestors helped her understand herself. Negative messages put us under a spell in childhood. Stories tell us we need a fairy godmother to break the spell.

6

NEGATIVE
MESSAGES

Negative messages are those words your family said to you that made you feel bad. No matter what the context, they transmit messages of shame, guilt and low self esteem.

Breaking the spell means sorting out the negative messages, defining, analyzing, and finally destroying them. We have incorporated them into our belief system—messages about ourselves, our behaviour, and our place in the world which we keep re-creating in a constant inner dialogue. When this dialogue changes, we are free to redefine ourselves.

Many parents seem proud of toughening up their children with negative messages. Then they say, "I was only teasing. Can't you take a joke?" However, children are incapable of seeing the joke when they feel hurt. Adults, when asked what they feel, respond, "I don't know; I don't feel anything. I just feel numb."

FRAN'S STORY

Fran, a competent but depressed 24-year-old writes:

> I once told my mom I didn't remember getting many positive messages when I was young. She listed all kinds of things about me that she was proud of, but said she never told me because she didn't want me to get a swelled head.

One of the rules in her family as she grew up was: Don't praise! However, she was often criticized and humiliated.

Mom criticizes my appearance, my choices, and my career in front of others. She tells stories about me as a child for the sole purpose of showing everyone how stupid I am. My mom and her mom too seem to think it's entertaining to humiliate me in front of the family—especially my father.

Fran knows her mother's role in her own family was the princess. Having attention lavished on her was very familiar. Since roles only change with conscious work, Mother's is still operative in her relationship with Fran. Fran plays the ugly duckling to her mother's princess. The unspoken messages Fran heard underneath her mother's criticisms were "don't be smart" and "don't be beautiful." A deeper message yet was "don't compete with me." There is room for only one princess in the family and the others are her subjects.

It may be much more subtle, but Fran's story has the flavour of *Snow White*, whose stepmother daily asks, "Mirror, Mirror, on the wall, who's the fairest of us all?"

In Fran's story it goes like this:

I have a picture of myself at four years of age with a friend at her birthday party. Recently I was looking at it with my mom. She said, "That's when you started getting fat!" I looked no different in size than my friend. We were both normal looking four-year-olds.

All my life my mother fussed about my weight. She took me to see a dietician when I was five. She constantly told me I was fat and said, "What do you think will happen to you when you grow up?"

The answer to me was obvious: I will become fat and ugly.

While Mother didn't want her daughter to compete and be better than she was, she still wanted her to look good—to show others what a good mother she was. This created an impossible dilemma, a double-bind, for Fran. She had to look good but not too good. She had to be smart but not too smart. She couldn't win. She could never be right.

> *"One message I got loud and clear, though she never put it into words, was that I was a mistake. I wasn't supposed to need her time or her love. In many ways she still tells me I'm not right, and when she's around I feel like I shouldn't exist."*

Historically Fran *was* a mistake. Her mother became pregnant before she and Fran's father were married. Because of Fran they had to get married, missing out on a courtship, a honeymoon, and time alone together for the first year or so. To Fran's mother, this was a hardship. They were young, emotionally unprepared, and financially strapped. Furthermore, Fran's mother came into the relationship unconsciously expecting to continue her princess role. Even though Fran had a warm relationship with her father, he wasn't often available. He remained Mom's loyal subject.

The earliest and most debilitating messages for Fran were: *don't be* and *don't need*. Most of her other messages can be superimposed on these. Another message that has had far-reaching effects throughout her life is *don't feel*. She says:

> *It was not okay to hurt or be sad. When I was little my mother chased me around the trailer so she could take a picture of me crying. When she showed me the picture she told me how stupid I looked.*

> *It was also not okay to be scared or angry. I used to wake up in the middle of the night, when I was three, feeling very scared. I would gather my courage together to make the long dash to my parents'*

room where my mom would tell me there was nothing to be afraid of and I was too old to get up at night.

Once my younger brother had gone into my room and made a huge mess. I went to my parents for help but they laughed in my face, telling me it was a funny thing to get angry about.

Fran suffered humiliation and emotional abuse as a child. Her spirit was nearly crushed and her trust in people was limited. Shame about her feelings and her very being are the outstanding themes of her life.

She survived by being a good, dutiful daughter. She had no choice but to learn the skill of walking a tightrope—being good enough but not too good at anything. She became another of Mom's loyal subjects.

I was useful in keeping her house clean and babysitting my younger brother. My mom told me she never had to worry about me because I was always so good.

Because Fran was neither heard nor seen when she felt bad, she always pretended she felt good. Fran's clear message from her mother: your feelings don't count; mine do.

Fran's negative messages were: don't be smart; don't be beautiful; don't compete with me; don't exist; don't need; don't cry; don't be scared; don't be angry; don't feel.

Fran is now involved in hearing, seeing and knowing what she needs. She is discovering that she has a right to have needs and to be here now—as she is. She is useful and competent at work, which is a familiar survival mode she developed growing up. Sometimes when she chooses not to be useful at home, she feels bad, depressed, unable to move. Feeling bad is an appropriate response to a bad situation. Fran's usefulness is both a denial and a protection against the despair of being unwanted—an emotional orphan.

Feeling bad is also part of healing; part of reconnecting with the lost parts of her child that were outlawed. Fran has created a safety net for herself today so she can do this work. It consists of an understanding mate, therapy, friends and a good work family. Most of all, she pays attention to herself.

We can set up a continuum of our fears and hopes about our negative messages. At the fear end, we think that getting to know them will be useless; there will be no end to the negativity and we'll be stuck in it for the rest of our lives. This is only our worst fear, not reality. It could be called our negativity about our negativity. At the opposite end, we hope that by working hard at healing we can wipe out our herstory and live *happily every after*. However, that's all it is—our highest hope.

The reality is somewhere in between. Getting to know ourselves gives us an opportunity to develop acceptance, flexibility, intuition, and the ability to make choices. On a very deep level we can feel faith in, and compassion for, ourselves.

Destroying negative messages takes some work. Naming them and making a list helps us contact covered-up feelings. By sharing the messages, we can understand what must be done to change them.

For some, finding the childhood messages may be difficult. If our parents are still alive, one of the best ways is to visit them specifically for the purpose of recovering those messages. If Mother still lives in our childhood home, so much the better. If not, a visit to that home may stir up long-forgotten memories. A walk from room to room may bring back the colour of the walls, patterns of curtains, placement of furniture, or even just snatches of feelings or events. Believe those flashes; our bodies and our unconscious do not lie or make up things that didn't happen.

Before visiting a parent or family home, we need to know what we want to achieve. As a child we longed for Mother to see, hear and affirm us. We may still hope for that today. Just by telling parents what happened to us as children, how we felt, how those events affect our lives and what we'd like from them now, we are affirming ourselves—whether or not they affirm us now. This requires much courage, for the shamed child within is still intimidated by our parents. Meeting Mother face to face can reduce that intimidation and strengthen us.

Eventually we can accept what Mother can give and stop hoping for the unattainable. At that point we can give ourselves what we need as well as ask for it from others.

Parents need to be retired from their roles as parents. Most parents are neither saints nor sinners; they don't intentionally set out to break our hearts. They are just ordinary people caught in a web of their own unconscious spinning, usually begun with their own upbringing.

> **NOTE:** If a parent was abusive, we may never be ready to go home and talk face to face. We may prefer to do it through a letter. If both parents are dead, we can still write them a letter or visit their graves and talk to them.

While this book does not focus on specific issues like physical or sexual abuse experiences, many books on these topics have been written.

Bad Feelings

A common complaint from women working on negative messages: "What's the point of dwelling on the negative? I felt bad enough as a kid and I don't want to feel like that again."

When we fail to acknowledge these feelings, we deny they exist. The energy we use to stay numb to protect ourselves from the feelings is negative energy. By releasing the negative energy, it is freed up for more positive use. It's as simple as that: expressing the bad feeling frees up energy to feel good.

Expressing the bad feeling doesn't mean dumping it on someone else. This only creates a vicious circle that eventually boomerangs back to ourselves. Instead, the feeling must be acknowledged, named and felt. Taking responsibility for our own feelings might sound like this:

"Right now I need to complain for 15 minutes, so please don't take it personally."

"I feel so irritable I just want to blame someone for how I feel, and you're the closest."

"I'm angry and need to blow up. It's not your fault."

The difference between blaming and taking responsibility is the I-message: I feel…, I'm angry…, I need…. Taking responsibility means acknowledging the need to blame. We can use one-liners like those above to let others know what we are thinking and feeling. We can discharge our feelings in a safe place with a safe person.

One woman set up a safe place at home by clearing out a pantry. She announced to her family, "This is now my yelling room. Sometimes when I'm mad I'll go in and yell. Don't worry about me. I'm fine. When I feel better, I'll come out again."

As children we were helpless to discharge negative feelings. We were our parents' captive audience. Our options were to stomp out of the house, stay in our room, swallow the hurt, be on our best behaviour, or numb out.

As adults, we want more from life than mere survival, numbing out. Fran discovered several ways to reduce her mother's toxicity. Since her mother is a constant complainer, Fran says:

Before I visit my mother, I tell her she has ten minutes to complain. That's my limit. After that I won't listen anymore. I know I have to be ready to leave if she doesn't respect my request. I feel like I'll actually get an ulcer if I don't do this for myself. It was hard at first, but it's getting easier. My mother tries to accommodate me. She even thanks me for coming to see her. That's a first.

Deborah's Story

Deborah, the mother of five grown children, is going home, not to discredit her mother's mothering, but to change the lifelong family messages. It was Dad who often told her, "Don't hurt your mother." Since Mother was the central focus of concern, and therefore the child of the family, Deborah's needs became secondary.

> When my children were becoming independent, I began wanting more from life. Someone suggested I go into therapy. I felt ready to do that. Up to that point, I had only felt love for my mother. During the years, I had talked with my parents about family and current events, but we talked of nothing personal.

> In therapy I contacted feelings of abandonment and rage. I deeply longed for connection and wept uncontrollably over the loss. I had never before been aware of Mother's rejection, of her not wanting me, her not being emotionally available. For the next two years, I allowed myself to feel anger toward her. Every time I was with her I thought of telling her how insecure and hurt I felt, how unwanted and unaffirmed by her. Although I began to call things more on my terms than hers, I never spoke up.

> On one visit, I was helping in the kitchen when Mom began to take things from my hands to do herself. Annoyed, I told her, "Come on, Mom, I'm a grown woman with five children. I know how to dry dishes and peel vegetables."

> Her response was, "How can you talk to me like that after all I've done for you?" I blew up. I yelled at her, "That is an illusion! An illusion! When have you done anything for me in all my married years? You have never helped me or my children." I began to cry and so did she. We held each other and cried. Afterward, I felt good. I felt tender towards her. We finally had connected.

Deborah later learned that her mother had aborted a baby before Deborah was born. When Deborah asked if she had tried to abort her as well, Mother sidestepped the question with, "Deborah, you've always been too sensitive." But Deborah persisted.

"Does that mean that I guessed right?" I asked my mother.

"Well, yes," she told me. "I did try to abort you, but it didn't work, and I'm glad it didn't."

"Mom, you've never told me you wanted me. I've always felt unwanted."

"You're a beautiful daughter and I love you."

Mother and I hugged warmly for a long time. Then I told her, "Mom, I've always longed to hear those words. They feel so good."

She said, "Surely you knew I loved you."

"No, Mom, I didn't. I need to hear it."

Deborah's negative messages: don't be, don't hurt me, don't need, don't be angry, don't be you, be a dutiful daughter.

Deborah's work continues. She keeps a journal, cares for and confronts her parents, pursues her chosen career, and constantly explores who she is becoming.

Looking at past negative messages is not a wasted lesson in futility. It is a positive way to release energy. Until we come to know what the roadblocks are, they run our lives. Knowing what these blocks are begins the process of release.

GUIDELINES

Talking With Mother
Set up a time to talk with Mother, face to face. (See Chapter 1 for suggestions.)

Finding Negative Messages
Get to know Mother's messages in the following ways:
> Participate in a therapy group.
> Listen to other's stories.
> Tell your story to a trusted other.
> Begin individual therapy.
> Make a list of verbal and non-verbal negative messages in your own childhood.

Drawing
Draw a floor plan of your childhood home. Label the rooms, place furniture, colour walls and carpets. Tack it up and keep adding details.

Writing
Write your memories, dreams and reflections in a journal.

Listing Messages
List all the negative messages you received as a child, especially from Mother. Use a separate page for each one.

- Say each one out loud to yourself several times, listening to the feeling in your belly—knots, butterflies, nausea, discomfort. Do you feel sad, mad, scared? If you don't know, just guess. Write your feelings under each entry.
- If a memory of a childhood happening emerges, let it affect you. Write it down.

- Double-bind messages are conflicting and keep us stuck. Notice those messages you received as a child, such as: keep quiet, speak up.
- How does each message affect your thoughts and actions today? Take lots of time for this one. Write down examples of things that happened recently. It may help to focus on the times you said "I know I should, but..." Pay attention to the "buts" in your life. Notice broken promises. Write down any injured animal dreams.
- What changes do you want to make now? Three to five years from now? Write them down on a separate page that you could stick on your mirror.

CREATING

Create a poster that includes all these dreams.

MORE WRITING

On separate sheets of paper, write the verbal negative messages you recall, similar to the following:

- Shame on you.
- I'll put you in a tub of cold water if you don't stop crying.
- I'll give you something to cry about.
- You're pitiful.

Do the same for non-verbal negative messages, like:

- Don't take care of yourself, only others.
- Don't have feelings.
- Don't talk about yourself.
- Don't be proud of yourself.
- Create a ritual to burn each of these messages.

Visualizing

Recall memories using a technique called visualizing.

- Find a comfortable place to lie down.

- Close your eyes and breathe deeply for a few minutes.

- Pick one of your childhood homes (preferably before you were 12) and imagine yourself walking up to the door, opening it and going inside.

- Take all the time you need to go from room to room, noticing all the objects that have an impact on you, especially the ones that are negative.

- Allow memories stirred by these objects to surface. Let yourself be affected by them.

- Be aware of what you feel.

- Notice the verbal and non-verbal negative messages connected to these objects.

- When you have completed your tour, open the door and say goodbye to all these negative influences in your life.

- Then close the door firmly and walk away from your childhood home.

- Gradually begin to come back to the present.

- Slowly open your eyes.

HIGHLIGHTS

- The roles we play in the family influence the kind of negative messages we receive.

- Some messages come later in our development; e.g., don't compete with mother. Some are earlier: don't be or don't need.

- Social and cultural events shape the kind of messages given: e.g. pregnancy before marriage, death or departure of a spouse, loss of another child.

- Many of us receive conflicting messages called double binds: e.g. be good but not as good as me.

- Survival tactics are necessary in a bad situation.

- A part of healing is knowing and feeling the bad situation. Another part is developing compassion for, and faith in, ourselves.

CHAPTER 7

Positive messages are like the three gifts
Demeter gave Persephone for her journey into
the underworld: a torch to light her way,
wheat for nourishment, and poppies to keep
her in touch with her intuition—her deeper
wisdom. This journey provides the
opportunity to burn the trash that does not
nourish us and to honour the gifts that lie
hidden and unclaimed.

7

EMPOWERING MESSAGES

All of us are born with power, purity and clarity. Somewhere in childhood we lose parts of ourselves as we absorb negative messages. In order to regain our birthright we must give up the burdensome family messages and traditions, and seek out the positive, empowering messages. If there are none, we can create those we wanted to receive. The greatest affirmation we can give ourselves is to *become* ourselves. In this way, the inner creative child who instinctively knows what to do can act spontaneously.

Sarah's Story

Sitting on her haunches on the kitchen floor beside the turned legs of the old elm table, four-year-old Sarah was colouring a picture. After she'd been working on it for quite awhile, her mother said, "Take a rest Sarah; you've been working so hard for so long."

"No," Sarah responded. "When I grow up I want to be just like Aunt Mary. She wouldn't stop. She would just keep on working." Aunt Mary was an artist who had recently introduced Sarah to the world of colour and design, completely entrancing the child.

Years later, as an adult, Sarah is immersed in focusing on the beliefs and behaviours she inherited from her family of origin. Several months ago she visited her parents to help contact the negative messages that had been passed down from earlier generations, some of which still affect her life today.

Now she feels ready to go home again to focus on the positive messages that were also transmitted to her. Studying her genogram gave her some clues about where to start, what to look for, what questions to ask. Looking back over several generations is like putting a wide-angled lens on her camera for a family reunion snapshot. Family beliefs and traditions come alive. Sarah's insights are more vivid than the too-narrow boundaries of the family in which she grew up.

From a dream she'd had only the night before, Sarah felt she was ready to explore more of her inner self through getting to know family roots.

> *I am looking in a store window. The store is full of beautiful, antique furniture, polished to a golden mellow patina. Chests and cupboards are uniquely designed with unexpected little drawers and doors. As I catch my breath in wonder, I exclaim, "Oh thank you, Aunt Mary, thank you!"*

Here was a female ancestor who had given her many treasures through her positive messages. How was she able to do this in a world filled with negatives?

Mary at age 12 had been put in charge of a household of ten children. A few years later, she fought with her father for the right to leave home to study nursing—not to get married as society decreed in those days. Mary was a woman who folks said knew her own mind, worked hard, and stood her ground.

On completing her training as a nurse, she married a wealthy man. Now someone else did the cooking and the house-cleaning. On an extended trip to Europe, Mary studied sculpture in Paris with two of the famous sculptors of that era. Her work became a lifelong love affair which she developed through long hours of work.

What Sarah learned from Aunt Mary:

- It is worthwhile to spend one's life energy following one's heart.

- Stand your ground when someone in the family says, "don't do that."

- To *want* is the birthright of every child.

On a sunny fall day filled with explosions of colour, Sarah drove up to the old farmhouse that once was home. Her father was uncharacteristically standing by the back door instead of reading his newspaper in his armchair. Usually she went to him for a hug. As she climbed out of the car after the long drive, the old man gave her a warm hug.

"Hey Dad, where's your newspaper?" Sarah joked.

"I've already read it. Not much in it anyway—it's all old news," he chuckled. "Come on in. Your mother's got dinner ready."

Mom was busy serving up the food, and *forgot* to hover over Sarah as she customarily did. As they sat down, Sarah was delighted to see the rose bridal wreath dishes she'd loved when she was very small. They were special to her Mother who had few beautiful things back then. Mom always used them for special events and special company—like Aunt Mary and Uncle John whom Sarah loved. Over the years these dishes had gathered an aura of love. Even as a little girl, Sarah had asked her mother if she might have them someday. The grown-up Sarah ran her fingers over the roses on her plate, looked up at her mother and felt how like a rose she was.

Mother never put herself forward, Sarah remembered. Instead she put herself *into* the many things she did well. When all her children had left home, she had gone back to teaching school. She loved learning and she loved children. This was her path with heart.

Thinking about the family history gathered in her genogram, positive messages from her grandmother and grandfather floated into Sarah's consciousness. Another of Mother's sisters also developed into a strong woman who found her place in a man's world and lived her life courageously. What were the messages her grandparents had instilled in their daughters?

It's okay to be successful.
It's okay to be an individual.
It's okay to have fun.
It's okay to follow your dreams.
It's okay to help each other.
It's okay to trust a higher being.
It's okay to trust each other.
It's okay to have money (or not).

This was a family that kept a chain letter going all their lives. In their letters they spoke their minds easily. They disagreed, they apologized, they recounted achievements, they affirmed each other. At family reunions every five years they played together, shared happenings, told stories about their mother and father, revelled in the next generation's offspring and achievements. Sarah learned what a healthy, down-to-earth bunch they were. This insight cast a different light on her mother as too much the martyr, too religious, too cheerful, too good.

Then Sarah's perceptions shifted to her father's family. With a jolt, she recognized that his family carried the *dark side* of human life. His family was more distant, more dysfunctional, more cut off from each other and their feelings. They were noted *for having tempers,* as she had read in a genealogy book. Dad's hostility, Sarah realized, is a family trait passed down from previous generations. It occurred to her that she needed both sides of these families. "I need the bright, cheerful, caring optimism of Mom's family and the anger, pain and hidden fear on Dad's side. Both these parts make me a whole person."

A long entry in her journal followed this last visit home. She wrote down her musings as they came to her—however rambling or jumbled. Since she wanted to expand the positive messages and turn down the volume on the negative, she made lists which created some succinct one-line messages. Looking back three generations greatly increased the positive possibilities available to Sarah.

Objects That Carried Positive Feelings For Sarah

Rose bridal wreath dishes
Embroidery by female ancestors
Grandmother's poetry
Mother's writings
Large, framed family photo of Mom's family in hall
Books Mom and Dad collected
Piano bought by Aunt Mary and Uncle John that Sarah
    loved to play
Paintings by family members

Parents' Positive Behaviours (past or present)

Dad greeting her at the door
Dad giving her a hug
Mom not hovering—doing too much for her
Mom and Dad asking about her—not her kids, her job,
    her husband
Mom sewing her first recital dress
Mom designing and sewing her wedding dress
Dad paying her music school fees

Messages From Women in the Family

You are talented.
Be passive and aggressive.
Be adventuresome.
Follow your heart.
Be successful.
Be independent.
Be an individual.

You have something to say.
Take a rest.
I'm concerned about your safety.
You are my beloved daughter.
Enjoy nature.
There is a higher power.
You have rights.
It's okay to play.
It's okay to create.
It's okay to dream.
I love you.
Fight for your life.

Messages from Males in the Family

You are sensual and sexual.
It's okay to enjoy money.
You have a wonderful temper.
It's okay to have fun.
Let her be.
Make friends.
You are "gutsy."
You have stick-to-itiveness.
Work hard for what you want.
You can do anything you want.

Positive Messages Sarah Wishes She'd Received and Can Now Give Herself

It's okay to make mistakes.
It's okay to be scared.
It's okay to be sad.
It's okay to be angry.
It's okay not to have answers.
It's okay to accept love as well as give it.
It's okay to enjoy.
Take your time.

Take care of yourself.

It's okay to be yourself.

On separate 3 x 5 cards, Sarah wrote affirming messages, from which she chose one to tape to her mirror each morning as a focus for the day. Transforming her ability to care for others into caring for herself has become a nurturing life task for her.

"Now I can retire my mother," Sarah realized.

SERENA'S STORY

The miracle of the human spirit is that it can burn stubbornly for many years despite a lack of encouragement, support, permission to exist, or unconditional love. Both our physical and emotional selves may appear starved, nearly dead, yet our spiritual body waits for renewal, to receive what we missed as children.

I was born an artist to two teenage parents who had no experience with the arts. As far back as I can remember I've always wanted to perform. Dancing, singing and acting are ways I bring to life the magic and truth of a divine presence within me. Performing is the most spiritually alive expression of myself.

Mom gave me a message that dancing and acting were just pastimes, hobbies. Performing was no way to earn a living. Even though I have never been able to make enough money doing what I love most, I have never stopped dancing.

Now at 40 I have the courage for the first time in my life to obtain an agent. During what others call a "mid-life crisis" I decided to pursue the career that I love. After all, what have I got to lose? They say "Life begins at 40!" And now Mom is ready to support my decision.

One of the great perks about being a therapist is seeing this miracle relived again and again in people's stories. Sometimes a person has trouble remembering positive messages. We use this protective memory as a catalyst to begin the journey in search of self.

Fran's Story Continues

I grew up feeling there was something wrong with me, that I was a mistake. What I wanted more than anything was to be told I was okay, wanted and loved.

As an adult I asked my mother, "Do you love me? Are you proud of me?" She would answer, "Yes, I love you. I loved you as a child, but I was afraid if I told you I was proud of you, I'd spoil you."

I still can't count on my mother or father to tell me I'm okay, although they are trying. It's hard for me to accept my husband telling me I am beautiful, loved and wanted. I'm always trying to figure out what his angle is. What does he want? or What did I do wrong?

To be truly free I must find the rightness and wholeness within myself. My task is to exorcise the poisonous parent within and build instead the loving place I needed as a child. I catch a glimpse of what it is to feel okay when I am creating—sewing or writing. I feel close to the freedom that I want most of all.

Fran's is quite an incredible task. In her family criticism is the way women talk to each other. Grandmother joined Mom in criticizing Fran. They both believed that praise corrupts. For Fran this meant ruling out any positive messages, which only magnified the negative ones. What courage is required to undo several generations of belief! Fran demonstrates that she really loves herself by her willingness to take on this gigantic task.

Victoria's Story

Learning family and community expectations is necessary for a child's development and survival. Once we learn this, the next stage of growth is to find ways to express who we are in the activities we love doing.

It took me years of having "my head in the sand" before I finally got back to doing what I love.

I grew up in a totally academic family who were all university professors. A rigidly hierarchical academic career had worked for them and that's what they expected for me.

I always wanted to be an artist, from the time I was three and received my first box of crayons. Every day I waited by the curb for the milkman's horse, Jack, to arrive. I'd give him a piece of bread and set to work drawing his great hooves to see if I could get the fetlocks just right.

I remember thinking how much I enjoyed drawing and how I wished I could make a career of art. But I knew I needed to be sensible. Grown up, I made several disastrous attempts at traditional universities, then finally enrolled in a Design and Craft Community College. My parents supported me financially, but I could tell they didn't really approve.

My family's beliefs about career choices were very strong. Shaking her head over the disaster of a wasted scholarship at a big American women's college, Mom said, "You could have been a curator in a New York gallery by now." I remembered thinking, "But Mom, I want to be the curated, not the curator."

Today I am an artist, doing what I love most to earn my living.

The greatest joy in life is quite simply to be yourself. But of course, it isn't always that simple. In Victoria's words, it may take years of *having your head in the sand* before you wake up.

In the fairy tale, Sleeping Beauty, we are told she slept for 100 years. Becoming your true self takes a very long time. At face value, the story suggests it took a prince from the external world to wake her up. In reality, her awakening came from the *prince* within herself. The prince symbolizes the courage to take chances, stand our ground and trust our intuition.

For most of us, the princely messages are buried so deep they are seemingly forgotten. However, they are still available for retrieval with a little work. The value of that work lies in the messages we dig out that empower us to take risks and carry out our dreams.

Sarah's Story Continues

I used to visit my Aunt Trudy and Uncle Bart nearly every summer when I was a child. I was afraid of my aunt who was a strict disciplinarian. If I ran to my uncle before she could catch me, he would keep her from spanking me. I felt intimidated by her and accepted by him.

When I was older, my aunt wanted me to play a recital at their home. I was scared of making mistakes. I'll always remember my uncle coming to my rescue. "Leave her alone. She's all right the way she is." My uncle was my protector and ally.

On my 40th birthday, my aunt sent me a critical card that said, "I don't like your hair colour. You don't look well. Have you seen a doctor lately? Don't go back to university. A friend of mine did and she failed. Happy birthday." I was mad enough to write her back: "I like my hair. I've never felt better in my life. And I'm going to university because that's something I want to do for myself. Furthermore, you've never told me you loved me and I really want to know if you do or not."

The next time I visited her, she sent everyone else out of the room on some pretext, then turned to me and said, "When I was growing up, we did things for people to show them that we loved them. I want you to know I do love you."

I'm glad I risked asking her. I'm sure she would never have told me otherwise. It helped me realize that I always need to check out my assumptions about people and to ask for what I want. I've always been glad I did it with my aunt before Aunt Trudy died.

Only we, as children, knew how we needed to be mothered. The same is true for us as grownups. Mothers make guesses about how to nurture based on their experience of being mothered, however good or bad that may have been. Mothering is a transgenerational process, an inner knowing passed down from one generation to another. If Mother wasn't mothered, she didn't learn how to mother her own children. This is a legacy completely out of our control. Add to this dilemma the knowledge that each of us is an individual with different needs.

Mothers can't be expected to guess right all the time. We need to let them off the hook. Today we are creators of our own destiny, not victims of fate. We can ask for what we need; the more specific the better.

If we are mothers, we can ask our children what they need rather than ignoring or controlling them.

Susie's Story

Seven-year-old Susie came home from school one day and tearfully ran to her mother. "What's wrong?" Mom asked.

"Jane was mean to me. She called me stupid and idiot all day."

"That was pretty mean," Mom replied. "Did you tell her that?"

"Mom, I'm not going to tell her that," Susie blurted out. "She would just do it more. Besides, you're not telling me what I want to hear."

"Okay, honey, tell me. What is it you want to hear?"

"I don't know," wailed Susie as she ran out of the room.

In a few minutes, she came back and told her mother, "Next time Jane calls me stupid I'm just going to act like I didn't hear her and I'm not going to play with her either."

You're a good thinker, dear," her mother responded. "I'm sure that's what you need to do."

"Thanks, Mom," called Susie over her shoulder as she ran outside to play.

Susie was thanking her mother for helping her know what she already intuitively knew. The child only needed to talk it through out loud. Most of us lose our intuition as we grow up. Healing begins with restoring it .

We could use a good fairy, a guide, to help us reclaim this inner wisdom. This is usually someone outside the family, although in our research we may feel attracted to certain ancestors, alive or dead, who can act as guides. However, the best guide of all is our emerging consciousness.

Exploring the family legacy provides a structure for peeling back the layers of psyche in order to reach our core self. If our family history is missing because of adoption, separation, death, or holocaust, we can uncover bits and pieces of stories to use in recreating it. We can use our intuition to make up and write down our personal myth.

Discovering our core self can be the gateway to deeper connections with our mother. In the previous chapter, Deborah and her mother never talked intimately until Deborah was middle-aged. The everyday task of peeling vegetables offered the key to begin a change in their relationship.

Like Deborah, the key for any of us is likely to be a common-place object or event. Fear of what lies beyond the gate is part of the dilemma that can halt our discovery. The antidote for fear is the willingness to risk, the willingness to allow ourselves the right to want.

Deborah's Story Continues

Often, the impetus to open our hearts to Mother is found in a crisis: an illness, death, disclosure of a family secret (incest, abortion, divorce), or the contents of an unfair will. When Deborah and her husband separated, she describes breaking the news to her parents.

For two months I didn't tell Mother about the separation, but Christmas was coming. I went to visit her and we sat in her kitchen. In a choked voice, I told her, "Harry has left."

My father put his hands over his face and moaned, "Oh no, oh no." My mother took my face in her hands and wept, "My beautiful daughter, my beautiful daughter."

Together we wept and connected. She assured me this was a beginning of a new and exciting life. I felt totally loving towards her. For years we had regarded each other from opposite poles. Now we have given up the polar positions through grieving together my divorce.

NERISSA'S STORY

Nerissa is in the midst of a satisfying life when she discovers she has breast cancer. This occurs at the time her mother is losing her fight with the same disease.

I was speechless with the horror of knowing that I had my mother's disease. It was the knowledge that she had affected me down to my very cells, that I had somehow co-created this manifestation, that made my bones crawl.

I was born 11 days after my father was killed in a car accident. Mother was the only parent I ever had. I was her "little ray of sunshine." I reasoned that if I played that role well, she would see who I am, come out of herself and love me.

My inner work has been to release myself from the unrealities of that role, the survival mechanism that has brought on the disease that scared me most. I have to let go trying to get something from my mother that she doesn't have to give.

Now she is dying. By walking the path with her, I have received many gifts that allow me to claim my womanhood in her presence, something I couldn't have done even a year ago. This week I took her to her doctor who invited her to listen to the truth—that she had entered the last phase of her life and all he could do was make her as comfortable as possible. "Nerissa," she said, "We are all dying. Some of us more slowly and some of us more quickly."

Mother and I went to her house to eat lunch. We cried together. I told her how brave she was to hear the truth. We talked about how she must now relinquish her outer life and call on her spiritual life that has always been important to her. She thanked me for being honest with her. "I feel so much closer to you," she told me; "I don't want any more from you. I just want to love you as you are."

My inner child basked in the glow that she finally saw me. My mother is affected by who I am. I felt freed in that moment to burn all my past karma and simply love this woman in her surrender to death.

I am not Mother's little ray of sunshine. I do have wisdom and strength that I have gained on my own path to becoming a woman. I choose to share whatever I have with my mother, with less and less desire to get something in return.

The experience I long for is my own acceptance of my inner unfulfilled child, as well as the accomplished adult that I am. I am fully human with my faults, resentments and weaknesses. I can access my own source of divinity, which will see me through helping my dear mother to die. Goodbye Mother, hello Woman.

Sarah, Serena, Fran, Victoria, Deborah, and Nerissa tried to do what others expected of them, but they never stopped wanting to do what they loved—wanting is the essential ingredient.

GUIDELINES

From our family heritage, we can choose what to keep and what to give up. Most of all, we can choose to create what is missing.

RESEARCHING

To create what is missing:

- List the positive messages you received or wanted to receive.

- Visit parents or relatives to look for the positive legacy.

- Plan a trip to your parents' birthplaces to fill in the missing links of genograms.

- Tape family stories of parents, relatives and friends.

- Find positive family keepsakes as visible reminders of positive connections.

- Make a video tape of research results.

- Create new snapshot albums of positive family experiences.

- Put together scrapbooks of what you want in life.

- Explore and experiment with ideas and activities that attract you.

VISUALIZING

- Do the same imagery as in Chapter 6 Guidelines, replacing the negative with the positive.

WRITING

- Write a story of your parents' lives up to the time that you were born.

HIGHLIGHTS

- Women tell their childhood life dreams, how they gave them up and how they later retrieved them.

- Discovering positive messages empower us to take risks and carry out our dreams.

- Our spirit can be quite indomitable. No matter how bleak life becomes, something told these women not to give up on themselves.

- The greatest affirmation is to continue to become. Choose to create what was missed.

- To want is the most essential ingredient to achieving a dream.

CHAPTER 8

As Persephone returns, Demeter throws a handmade cape of white crocus around her daughter's shoulders. They cry and laugh and hug and dance. The cape of flowers becomes a beloved herloom for Persephone. "Herloom" is a metaphor for women's power handed down from generation to generation. China tea sets, everyday wooden spoons, tattered books, hand-crocheted afghans and pearl necklaces are the repositories of female traditions.

8

HERLOOMS

Separating and staying separated throughout their lives is the male model of defining maturity—individuation. This patriarchal tradition of autonomy and separation is misleading for women. Thanks to the work of such women as Alice Miller, Jean Baker-Miller and Carol Gilligan, we know that women's identity is forged through relating with others, not standing alone.

"Herlooms" link us to our evolution. Since herlooms are the repository of female traditions, they take on a special significance for us.

Women pass down our favourite recipes, quilts, china, silver, linens, pearls—family herlooms—to our daughters. Sometimes they are things made by our own hands, or by mothers and grandmothers—imbued with love and polished to a lovely soft luster over the years. It is as though our female kin live on in these articles of faith. Of course, this can only be true if our hearts are open to receive this power from our ancestors. The blessing of those who have gone before is ours if we choose to accept it.

Jackie's Story Continues
There are women who, early in childhood, disconnect from their mothers, whether a birth, adoptive or surrogate mother. Jackie has been asleep to her feminine self. When she awakens

to the emptiness and rage inside, she is faced with a choice: remain stuck in bitterness or swim through the rage to the opposite unknown shore that represents healing and self-knowledge.

Jackie was disconnected, not only from her mother, but from herself as well. Now she is engaged in getting to know herself. She is halfway to the opposite shore. Women's handiwork, which Judy Chicago so brilliantly illustrated in The Dinner Party, is the living bridge over the fear, uncertainty and rage that separates women from women throughout the ages.

Jackie reconnects with her female kin through the household belongings handed down from generation to generation. Examining these herlooms and the family herstory strengthens her sense of identity.

A slim, dark, anxious woman, Jackie sits forward in the therapy chair, as she reminisces about her roots and in particular, her memories of her mother. Six months ago, she phoned her therapist to report a crisis in her relationship with her mother. After that, the therapy became intense. Her journal is filled with her feelings of sadness and anger. An enormous burden has been lifted from her shoulders.

I can see the light at the end of the tunnel. I feel I can see Mother as a person, a woman behind the Mother Mask.

I remember as a child of 10, crouching on the landing between the railings of the upstairs bannister, listening to the laughter of my mother's bridge club. I longed to taste those tea sandwiches, dainty asparagus and watercress rolls. After all, I had helped to make them that day in the warm kitchen.

These middle-aged friends of my mother gathered in her parlour with its freshly polished, lemon-oiled furniture and starched, crocheted armrests. The table center had been troublesome! Mother's confidence wavered here—how to arrange the peonies I had picked from our garden? Mom, feeling increasingly frustrated, allowed me to fuss with the posies. How proudly I bent over the crystal bowl, sticking the stems into the wire mesh.

"You had a way with flowers, and mother was all thumbs," commented the therapist. "You are different from your mother. What you and your mother did not know or acknowledge is that it is okay to be different and to share similarities. Some daughters and mothers can seize the points of difference to encourage young daughters to grow into their own uniqueness."

In the beginning of therapy, Jackie had felt that her own ambitions were squashed and had been laid aside many years ago. Today, she proudly continues her recollections of the bridge party.

Aunt Ida's oval crocheted doily crowned the walnut tea table. Aunt Ida was my mother's surrogate mother. Mom, as a young girl, boarded with her during the winter months when the farm roads were impassable for school children. Placed on the doily were the flowers in a crystal bowl. Matching cups and saucers were lined up in a linear pattern on one side, bowing to the tea sandwiches and napkins on the other side. The "eats" were laid out under the shadow of the silver tea service which graced the altar.

The therapist visibly started at the word altar, an unusual word to use for the dining room table. She had heard women pouring out their treasured memories of how Mother had stood ironing or baking, or kept house with a grace and care that dignified the simple household tasks. This is not to deny that domestic work was often felt to be drudgery. However, the sacred aspect of women's work had surfaced here as it had in other therapy sessions. Other women had sat in the therapy room and told of their pride in grandma's needlepoint and quilts. A christening or tea party was a special occasion to celebrate women's crafts. Homemade preserves and hand-painted cups were displayed where all could take pleasure in them. The table/altar was a feast for body and soul around which friends and family gathered. Women of yesterday unknowingly proclaimed their feminine identity by the preservation of their domestic handiwork.

To add to memories of her roots, Jackie visited her cousin, Rachel, in Florida, a long way from the small Ontario town where Rachel was raised:

> *Rachel took me by the hand to show me her collection of my mother's family treasures. We strolled through her living and dining rooms. She would stop and pick up a cup here, a photo there, retelling the family stories she had heard as a child. I had that electric experience that the room was peopled with our common ancestors.*

Her therapist was moved by the image of Jackie identifying with her female kin through the herlooms Rachel had shown her. "We can change *heirlooms* to *herlooms* when we are talking of our female treasures," she offered.

Jackie, an only daughter, would pass on to her only daughter the herlooms that carried rich memories of her own female identity. It is not only the valued antiques in which this wealth abides. Everyday china, linen and wooden spoons can hold special significance for daughters, and reflect our female bond. Women need to reclaim their identity. Often it is woven into the female crafts and objects passed on from mother to daughter.

As Jackie shared her flashbacks, she became aware that they were powerful clues pointing the way to her emerging identity.

> *I remember the order and beauty of a well-set tea table; the handwork of a smocked dress with tiny rosebuds; the shining bottles of freshly made chili sauce in the spice-filled kitchen. It wasn't until I turned 40 that I realized I hadn't cared for my*

*grandmother's quilt—it was torn by the dog and by the rough play
of the children. Unknowingly, I had neglected the wealth of my
roots.*

Jackie's memories of childhood were her attempts to reclaim her lost heritage. Jackie had lost touch with the world of
women; she had lost the primary relationship with her mother;
she had lost herself.

To all appearances, she was a successful mother to four
teenage children, wife of an ambitious, kindly husband, and a
competent community volunteer. She was on friendly terms
with everyone in her family, well ensconced in her female roles.
Yet she was going through the motions and feeling an emptiness and unhappiness she couldn't explain.

As Jackie continued her work, unearthing seeds of her
discontent, the themes of her family began to emerge:

*My grandmother was a workhorse on the family farm. The rules
my mother passed on to me were: "Look after the men because they
work hard outside. Serve them first from the Sunday roast. Choose
the choicest cuts for them—what's left is for the women." I got the
message very clearly that women's work is unimportant and
secondary to men's.*

*Why were everyday domestic tasks devalued as being women's
stuff? I was the only daughter with four brothers. As a girl I didn't
consider my mother's tea table important. I was scornful of the
everyday clutter with which mother surrounded herself. I ridiculed the chaos of the junk drawer where Mom put balls of string,
elastic bands tossed in confusion, a screwdriver, broken scissors
and many unrecognizable objects only Mother could identify. I
vowed then that when I grew up I'd never allow my kitchen
drawers to become so untidy.*

Guess what appeared over my years of keeping house? An oddly assorted miscellaneous drawer—a no-name collection of odds and ends. Until this moment, I hadn't connected this with my mother. Now it feels like a comfortable, warm memory.

Jackie continues to piece together her heritage. Alike and dissimilar, daughters and mothers are in relationship. Growing up and away from Mother, from parents, is the journey of maturation towards ourselves—individuation. The journey for females begins by connecting with Mother, then moving away from her towards who we are becoming, and lastly, reconnecting in a mature way, as equals.

GUIDELINES

Connecting with Female Ancestors

Take a walk through your apartment or house. Look at what you have collected, your furniture, the colours you have chosen. Do some things seem more loved than others? Do some attract your attention? If so, why?

Write down your thoughts and feelings while you have the special cup or plate or afghan in your hand, or while you sit in that rocking chair. Are your female ancestors present in that object? Describe the feelings you have.

Looking at Family Albums

Find pictures of your mother—as a baby, a young girl, as a young woman. Let the pictures speak to you.

Then find a picture of yourself at each of these ages, and let them speak to you.

Compare the pictures by laying the age-appropriate snaps side-by-side. What are your reactions? Note the brooches, hairpins, the christening robe or dress. Does anyone in the extended family recognize these items? Know of their whereabouts?

Visiting Relatives

Phone or write a letter to a relative who might be able to show you some of their prized family herlooms. Ask them to tell you the stories about these kinfolk. Ask questions like "What was Grandmother Matilda really like? What kind of life did she have? How did the family treat her? Can you recall the rings she wore in that anniversary picture?"

Researching

Research trunks, chests, cartons, the attic, basements, spare rooms. Many old families still have boxes of family photos, odds and ends, that may not be just junk. Some may have pitched out all the memorabilia due to lack of space or interest. There is almost always a family historian who likes to save family mementos. Visit her; connect with her; gather information from her.

Sharing

Invite a friend with whom you can share your information about family herlooms to visit your home. Offer to reciprocate with her if she is interested.

Taking Photos

Select certain herlooms to be photographed. Take time to set up and display them for a closeup picture. Print labels describing each item and approximate dates it was made and/or in use, and by whom. Let the pictures speak to you. Display them for friends or put one under your pillow.

Meditating

Do you remember the mother of your childhood? What did she look like? What did she wear? What did you dislike about her? What did you like about her?

Visualizing

Return to your childhood home: what can you see in your bedroom? In the kitchen? Visit your mother's special space, if she had one— her bedroom, her sewing room, her writing desk—wherever she spent private time.

HIGHLIGHTS

- The patriarchal tradition of defining maturity in terms of autonomy and separation is misleading. Women forge their identities through relating to others.

- A woman's path to maturity lies in moving away from parents, toward herself. Then she can reconnect with loved ones in new relationships of interdependence.

- Women's handiwork, an important repository of family traditions, may aid in reconnecting. Herlooms link us to our evolution.

- Passed down from grandmother to mother to granddaughter, they take on a special significance for women.

- Everyday tasks can be carried out with a sense of the sacred as the familiar objects are lovingly used and re-used.

- We can receive the power of ancestors when we use their things: recipes, quilts, linens, jewelry, dinnerware.

CHAPTER 9

The work roles for Demeter and Persephone were well-defined. Demeter was the giver of crops; Persephone was the symbol of new crops. Demeter's work was to teach mortals how to plant, cultivate, harvest and store grains. For women in early civilization, agriculture represented life restored. In the underworld, Persephone's work was to renew the spirits. Together, they offered ongoing life to the earth.

9

WOMEN'S WORK: HEARTH AND HOME

Women carry the heritage of generations of women's lost ambitions which were submerged. These lost dreams cause bitterness, frustration and negative patterns, such as over-working, over-caring, and over-compensating.

Women's work has undergone major change in the last 30 years. Back then, women going out to work were blamed for damaging children's development, men's egos and the nation's economy. Now, financial necessity sends both partners out to earn a salary. Studies show, however, that when women work outside the home, they often are still the sole homemaker and caregiver.

Putting energy into a system that doesn't work for us creates discomfort, deprivation, depression and, if continued long enough, illness. This is negative stress. Positive stress would be using energy to create more of what we want. This may be a difficult task, but is a positive way to use energy created by stress.

Since work is a vast topic, this chapter charts only a few conflicts and choices voiced by women.

Sarah's Story Continues

Sarah is exploring a gnawing dissatisfaction with her life. As she does, a path with purpose begins to unfold for her, little by little. Sarah is asking herself some very difficult questions.

Why am I in this world? What do I want to do? How do I need to live so I will feel fulfilled when I die?

Up to now, my energies have been consumed in providing a home for my husband and daughters. Friends and family tell me, "You've got it all," or "you're a lucky woman," or "you should be happy with your life."

So why do I have this sick feeling—this gnawing in my innards that won't go away? No matter what anyone else says, I have to find out what's wrong.

Sarah has questioned her own role growing up in her family, as well as her mother's role in her family. She has made several visits home to gather information about her genogram and her family map. She recorded in her journal both the negative and positive messages, spoken and unspoken, that she received as a child, sharing some of these with each parent separately on different occasions.

"Mom, when I come home I'd like you to go about your work. Hovering over me makes me feel like I'm still a little girl and I can take care of myself now," I told my mother. "Dad, when you come outside to greet me and give me a hug, I feel valued and loved by you," I told my dad. Another time, when I asked to have lunch alone with Dad, Mom made a big fuss, "What do you want to do that for?" Dad responded, "Your mother feels left out." I told them, "I want to know each of you as people, not only as my mom and dad."

Out of Sarah's excitement in studying her family system

came her decision to train for a career. When Sarah grew up during the Great Depression, the family's biggest concern was mere survival. There was no time or money for anything else— especially looking at how their system was functioning. Today Sarah wants to change her role in the family.

However, resistance to change is strong. Her family and friends stopped telling her to be happy, and started saying things like, "If you leave your marriage, we won't support you." And still another, "If you open the barn door and gallop into the meadow, you may find the barn door locked when you come back." Or "You should be the little woman behind your man."

Coming home exhausted after two days of training, she was met with silence from her husband. Sometimes while writing essays, her husband slammed doors in the kitchen as he did the dishes. It reminded her of a minister's sermon she'd heard once about "A woman's place is in the kitchen."

As Sarah steps out of the kitchen into the world, some people say, "You better know your place, little woman!" She is frightened at her own audacity in breaking family rules and society's mandates.

"Don't change!" is the threatening message. Regardless of her fear, Sarah knows there is no turning back. Remembering how depressed she was earlier, and how empowered she feels now, she knows she is on the right path.

Instinctively, Sarah knew she needed all the help she could get to stand her ground. She wrote down affirmations like "I'm a gutsy woman", or "I want the highest good for myself", or just "I'm ok" on cards that she taped to her mirror, saying one of these to herself each morning as she combed her hair and brushed her teeth.

Sarah continued with her career change and joined a support group. She surrounded herself as much as possible with the positive messages she'd always wanted to hear and limited her exposure to negative messages.

Studying her genogram, Sarah focused on the career choices of women in her family. She unearthed a family secret about her mother that no one had ever mentioned before. Nellie, Sarah's mother, was a small-boned, fine-featured woman of delicate health. She married a farmer against her family's wishes. Although she was a hard worker and devoted to her children, she received little nurturing from her marriage. After the birth of her third baby, Nellie visited a divorced brother, hoping for support to leave the marriage and build her own life. Instead he exhorted her with: "Your place is with your husband and children." Resigning herself to her fate, Nellie returned home to bear two more children, Sarah being the last.

A woman better know her place! That's the same message my mother received. It wasn't until I grew up that my mother at last pursued her own life. She loved teaching and she loved children, so this became her path with purpose until she was forced to retire at 65. During these years, she was a livelier, more vital person. Maybe she was a fun person when she was young. I wish I'd known her then.

Sarah resolved to get to know her mother better now—not as the resigned mother she remembered, but as the playful little girl she had once glimpsed. She researched other female family members and saw that her mother's sisters' choices were very different from her mother's. After helping to raise her siblings, Nellie's older sister studied art.

Nellie's younger sister, Trudy, was an early feminist who became one of the first female school principals. Neither of her sisters had children; instead they followed their own paths. Sarah never had a sense that they regretted their choices. In fact they remained lively, fun-loving women all their lives!

Although the gutsy women from this family had carved out careers for themselves, Sarah knew most women of their era had no choice but to become wives and mothers. This was the only route acceptable to family and society. Some of these women found second careers within the home. For many generations, these were:

- Best cook in the county
- First prize winner in needlework at the autumn fairs
- Green thumb of the community
- Writer in the local magazines
- Sought-after singer in church choirs
- Painter of flowers, wildlife or landscapes
- Church organist
- Hospital auxiliary chair

At coffee klatches Sarah's friends told stories about their own mothers:

Susan: "One day I opened the door to the store room, and there was my mother sitting on the floor, surrounded by boxes of mementoes. She was crying. I knew she was remembering her lost youth. This was her work and I couldn't comfort her, so I closed the door quietly. But I'll never forget the look on her face."

Ann: "I came home from school one day and there was my mother ironing clothes and crying like her heart would break. I didn't know what to do either, so I went out and picked her a bunch of daisies."

Almost everybody remembered a similar story of her mother's pain—the betrayal of the lost little girl she once was, the pain of sacrificing her own dreams for the greater good of the family.

In a society loyal to patriarchal values, women's work is often trivialized, ridiculed, denied, and even vilified. Much of their visibility is wiped out in the daily work of washing, scrubbing and polishing. Only their memory remains, glowing with the patina of age, in the hearts of those who love them.

In the previous generation, Sarah saw her mother and sisters struggling to be more autonomous, more recognized in a society that treated women as possessions under the control of men—men like Sarah's grandfather who built and furnished his house and decided on having a family of ten before finding a bride. However, these three sisters, daughters of this grandfather, preferred to be known for their own accomplishments rather than to live through someone else's. They cleared a path through virgin territory for the next generation.

There are many ways women choose to individuate such as: changing careers in mid-life, beginning a career after the children are grown, becoming a mother later in life, or not becoming a mother, choosing not to marry, exploring how we want to be the same or different from our mothers. The real work underlying all of these choices however, is that of equalizing the power between ourselves and our parents.

Donna's Story

A highly successful lawyer in a predominantly male profession, Donna felt that she was in danger of a heart attack. A vivacious, witty, mother of two, she usually worked a 14-hour day at the office. This was the price for being as good as a man at a man's job in a male firm. Donna had trai*ned* for this career as a very young girl, always fighting her mother's battles with her father.

She became known as a tiger in the courtroom. Fighting everyone else's battles in the courtroom was just a change of locale from the family kitchen. At the same time it was a choice that brought approval from a difficult, critical, and sometimes abusive father. He had looked to her brother to be the successful professional—to achieve what he had been unable to do. Since her brother refused to live Dad's life, Donna fulfilled his dreams.

Her choice had the potential of pleasing both parents. She was fulfilling Dad's dreams and doing Mom's individuation work. Mom was helpless, so Donna was strong. Mom stayed in the kitchen, so Donna went out into the world. Mom needed rescuing, so Donna rescued.

In her over-responsible, workaholic lifestyle there was no time for Donna to come home to her inner self. She had never been the little girl picking flowers in the field with her friends. Now her heart was warning her that the time had come to learn to play—to focus on herself for the first time in her life.

After a sabbatical, Donna chose to return to the same profession. She listens to her heart more now. She has stopped being over-responsible and started being self-responsible, no longer working 14-hour days.

GEORGIE'S STORY

Georgie is a single mother, a risk taker who is pushing out the edges of what has been traditionally acceptable for women.

I've always kept a tool chest in my linen closet. I like knowing how to build and fix things. It makes me feel strong, capable and confident. Finally I trained as a carpenter because the government was offering free courses and subsidized day care to women entering non-traditional jobs. Besides I thought I'd like it.

Growing up I was called a tomboy because I liked to play with the boys. Later, seeing my mother's resentment about her role as wife and mother, I realized women get the short end of the stick and a lot less respect than men. So I tried hard to be one of the guys. That's partly why I chose "males only" activities, like carpentry, playing bass in a rock band, and playing pool. I tried to be as good as a man. And although I received attention, both good and bad, I was never really accepted as one of the guys. Finally I gave up trying.

As a single mother, Georgie juggles a formidable time schedule between day care, child care, job and house maintenance. In spite of the crushing task of fitting into a male occupation in a male world, she finds time to re-create herself. She reflects on her unique purpose in this world, "Because I no longer have to struggle to see myself as worthy in others' eyes, I have come closer to enjoying who I am and what I do."

When women leave home to go to work, we simply transfer our family system to the work environment. We recreate what is most familiar to us—our family. This is such a well-known phenomenon that systems theorists have labelled it *isomorphism.*

We may not notice what's happening since we're living on automatic pilot. We find ourselves relating to the boss as a mother or father, a co-worker as a sister or brother. We continue to try to live up to our parents' expectations. If *scapegoat* was our role at home, we may find ourselves singled out for blame at work. If we were the family's *heroine,* we constantly rescue people and dedicate ourselves to good works.

As the third daughter in her family, Georgie the carpenter tried to be the son her parents never had. While she is competent in her work, she is not *one of the guys.* Her life task is to give up fulfilling her parents' dreams and to follow her own.

Nerissa's Story Continues

In Chapter 7, Nerissa told of her horror at contracting her mother's disease. They had been *best buddies,* with Nerissa's job to be Mother's sunshine. Nerissa had taken on the role of her father who died shortly before she was born. Her survival depended on keeping the remaining parent around to take care of her.

Now, as an adult woman with a debilitating disease, Nerissa is using her situation as an agent for change.

The most important thing I received from a healer was this: "Nerissa, this is the rest of your life in terms of your body. You must slow down. You must rest, sleep for several hours every single day. How you heal yourself now, after this first attack, affects the remainder of your physical existence."

My response to "sleep for three hours" was ,"Impossible. I have my children, the new baby, my husband, my practice, my country life, my house, my gardens, my horses, my presidency of the school board, the rest of my life! Impossible." I was being told to give up my life as it was to fit the uncompromising necessity to make room for my life as it is.

I chose to step off the road of my previous expectations into the uncharted territory of my inner self. Slowly I divested myself of the outer responsibilities. I hired help with the children. My husband began to answer his own needs. I gave up nursing the baby and presiding over the school board.

For the first few months I walked into my office at home like I was facing a firing squad. Relatively soundproof from the rest of the family, it offered shelter where I could devise rituals to ease the transition from "I must keep going" to "I must rest and heal." In the absence of ordinary life and in the presence of an extraordinary life, I began to plumb the depths of my soul—an area I had never had courage to face even after years of therapy and spiritual practice.

If I am not just a victim of life but co-creator of my illness (however unconsciously), I reasoned, then I am also co-creator of my healing. Hardest of all was replacing the notion of "curing" myself with the ongoing process of "healing" myself, no matter how my body outwardly responded, for better or for worse.

After deeply sleeping away the three hours of my allotted time, I evolved into practices using meditation, breath, sound and subtle movements that are now part of my own professional work.

Most importantly, I took a major dive into the real me, the me that lives beyond the narrow definition I had given myself before my illness. Now I don't know how I ever lived without time woven into my days and nights to reflect and just be in my own waves and rhythms. I intend to go right on healing myself. This has become a way of life for always.

The most unusual outcome of Nerissa's illness was permission for her to stop doing all the extraneous busy work. It is the busy-ness that distracts us from what our hearts want us to do. Understanding that this self-care is women's birthright is a stunning revelation to many of us. Overnight, clarity about each person's expectations and boundaries became an important value for Nerissa's family. She reorganized her life around the needs for uninterrupted sleep at night and three hours' rest during the day. When her young child complained, "Mom, you're always tired," she responded, "That's the kind of mother you have now."

Sometimes a personal transformation requires a change of work, perhaps a dramatic one. Often, it simply means changing focus from performing to meet others' expectations to expressing who we are.

Evelyn's Story

Evelyn is a 40-year-old professional who keeps a dream journal. She recorded the following dream:

Two beautiful creatures are swimming in the university pool, a lovely dolphin and a dark, sleek shark, both about the same size. As I watch, the shark viciously attacks the dolphin, attempting to kill it. The shark is disgusted by this people-pleasing wimp with whom it is forced to share quarters. The dolphin is horrified, mystified because it only wants the shark to like it.

Some young men in the pool gallery attack the shark under the pretext of saving the dolphin. I suspect they are more interested in the fun of the kill than in the welfare of the dolphin. I am very upset and manage to prevent the slaughter. After all, the shark has a right to live too. It seems wrong to condemn it for being what it is by nature.

Both animals have been saved for the moment. I am left with the dilemma of finding a place or a way for these two beings, so different from each other, to co-habit in some degree of peace or at least tolerance.

In many ways, this dream seems like the story of my life. How can I be playful and loving and, at the same time, express the dark aggressive side that is more primitive and dangerous? I admire both sides of myself. There must be a way to forge a strong and lasting alliance, one that would be apparent in my personal relationships as well as in my work life. This is proving to be quite a task, one that I suspect will always challenge me."

At first Evelyn believed she would have to change her profession to save her shark self. This was a difficult decision since she received much positive attention and approval for her performer self. While her job exacted a high price in terms of stress, it also provided many perks.

Evelyn researched other jobs as she explored the people-pleasing silver dolphin part of herself and the dark, sleek shark part. How could she accept the qualities of both these creatures? She concluded she could stay in the same profession and find a way to please herself more and others less. During her search of many years, she worked on the primary life triangle—mother, father and herself. Being the only child intensified this triangle.

Many women contributors to this book have commented on ways they re-cycled their relationship with Mother in their work. They consciously changed the wounding patterns with Mother, e.g., too invasive, critical, cold, or distant, into ways to heal themselves. By going into the hurt, they found ways to transform it. We may spend years re-creating our childhood before we are ready to change.

Cybil's Story

Cybil re-created her family dynamics in her work situation. Out of awareness of her childhood strengths and weaknesses, healing began. Cybil changed her rigid boundaries against her mother's invasiveness into more flexible ones that allow her to fulfill a longing for more satisfying relationships.

I confess I fashioned myself to be more like my father than my mother in my choice of work. My relationship with my mother was stormy from as far back as I can remember. She was invasive and had great difficulty hearing and responding to my needs. She would pepper me with questions and then distort my meaning, much as a deflecting mirror works opposite to a reflecting one.

These are not the qualities one would care to re-create. What I have concluded is that since Mother was so invasive, I developed a strong sense of boundary, like a wall, and was really quite afraid of people. I think I chose my kind of work to learn how to be in relationship with others.

My journey has been to move towards people, to become an open human being. My own healing occurred over the years as my clients taught me in many wonderful ways how to be with them.

Ever since I can remember, I daydreamed about love and close-ness. This longing eventually manifested itself in my choice of career, one that is rewarding for me. I continue to change my relationship with my mother by setting firm boundaries around her invasiveness. When I send clear, non-critical messages to her, she responds. I am aware that as I see myself differently, I simply relate differently to my mother.

Mother can be the most powerful agent of change. Working on relationship with her is interchangeable with working on all other relationships. As this work progresses, we are peeling back layers of our own psyche to reach our core.

GUIDELINES

WRITING

- List negative family messages about work, such as:

  A job's a job: it puts bread on the table.
  A good person is a hard worker.
  Daydreaming is a waste of time.
  What makes you think you can do that?

- Go back into childhood. Attach adjectives to each of the following:

  List childhood dreams.
  Honour each dream; discard none.
  List good things about each.

  What were your favourite toys?
  Describe them.
  Describe your feelings about them.

  What were your favourite books?
  Who were your heroes or heroines?
  Why did you admire them?

  What were your favourite play themes?
  What was exciting about them?
  What did you learn about yourself?

  What were your hobbies?
  What did you like best about them?
  Are you still interested in them today?
  Think of these adjectives as describing yourself.

CHANGING WORK HABITS

- For those with a pattern of working long hours, leave work an hour earlier.

- Go to work an hour earlier and quit an hour earlier. Or go to work an hour later and quit an hour later. Negotiate with someone to cover your desk or take care of the children for an hour. Use this hour (morning or evening) for exercising, meditating, sleeping, painting or something rejuvenating.
- If you usually work or do errands over lunch, determine to take that time for walking in the park, sitting on a park bench with eyes closed, or observing nature. Talk with the birds!
- After lunch, you could lie down behind your desk with a newspaper over your head. Learn to go into a relaxed state for 15 minutes. Take relaxation classes if necessary.
- Have plants, flowers, paintings in your work space.
- Set up objects with special meaning to induce the feeling you'd like to have more frequently. A watch can remind you each hour to focus on this feeling.
- Specify times when you are not available for interruptions and times that you are.
- A closed door or an open door can be a reminder of these boundaries.
- Notice high stress periods each day. Make allowances for them.
- Be willing to leave some work unfinished at the end of the day.
- Tell others how you work best: what you will or won't do. Practice ways of saying this in a factual non-threatening manner, using "I" statements.
- During high stress periods, wear a small pocket recorder with earphones to listen to relaxing music for 15 minutes.
- Negotiate equal housework and child care with an appropriate person.
- Each person can make extensive lists of jobs done daily, weekly, monthly, yearly. Choose a fair division. A pen-

alty for neglect might be: that person gets to do all the jobs the next week. Write out your agreed-upon job descriptions.
- Make time every day to visualize an ideal work situation. When ready, begin making small changes.

Meditating
Every day for a month meditate on:
What would be a path with heart?
or—What would be a path with purpose?

Visualizing
- Choose an undisturbed time and space. Take 5-10 minutes to breathe, taking in a little more each time until you are breathing all the way from pelvis to shoulders.
- Begin to visualize the room in which you'd like to work. Picture all the details: colours, furnishings, books, pictures, decorations, music—everything.
- Take all the time you want.
- Slowly come back to the room. Draw and colour a picture of your imagery. Put this picture in the back of your mind. When you see a tangible object that fits this picture, you will recognize it.
- You will know when you are ready for it to happen

Drawing
Change can occur only when it's possible to see how a system operates and what your roles are. Draw a map of your work family to make this visible.
- Follow instructions for the family map at the end of Chapter 2.
- Notice similarities.
- What role do you play?
- Who is Mother? Father? Siblings?
- Who are allies, enemies or strangers?

- What does it mean to be male? Female?
- Who wields the most power?
- How would you change your role?
- Compare it to your family map.

Changing Careers

Write a complete game plan starting with the first, easiest and simplest steps. Research your areas of career interest :
- Read about those that interest you.
- Interview people already working in that field.
- Take courses to prepare you for this career.
- Do you want to work for someone else or start your own company?

If you want to work for someone else:
- Read a company's annual reports.
- Interview managers of departments that interest you (purchasing, accounting, marketing, production, administration, etc.)
- Talk to people in competitive companies and in trade organizations.
- Contact trade organizations.
- Let people know you are available.

If you want to work for yourself, consider the following:
Finances
- What realistic amounts will you need for the first five years (supplementary income or business investment)?
- What people might invest in your idea?
- If you wish to create a company, who might offer financial support?
People
- Do you wish to work alone?
- Consider working with 2-4 people (not 3. In a triangle, someone always is on the outside).

- Who is compatible with you?
- Who has the skills you need?
- What are each person's strengths and weaknesses?
- How will you handle conflicts?
- Write job descriptions.

MARKETING

- How will you sell your product (or your services)?
- What markets are presently available?
- How is your product/service different?
- Who will use your product/services?

Add to this list as much information as you can.

HIGHLIGHTS

- Family, friends and society try to tell us how to be.

- Each of us needs to find our own path with purpose.

- Family and friends tend to say "don't change." We need to learn to ignore them and mother ourselves.

- Change is difficult; it takes time.

- Take a look at the choices female ancestors made. Note the choices friends make. What choices are your daughters making?

CHAPTER 10

Reclaiming her core self is the purpose of Persephone's journey into the underworld. The torch which lights the darkness keeps her focused on this task. It represents what she wants from life: to be more creative and loving. Living more from her core is worth the journey.

10

OUR OPTIONS IN THE RELATIONSHIP

Demeter and Persephone struggled to achieve a balance with their life work and with each other. Demeter sat at the well and mourned. Persephone explored her history and her work options. These were appropriate choices for each of their life stages.

There are many steps along the way, starting with the decision to begin. Following are nine major options which are practical, along with specific suggestions to help get started.

The Nine Major Options are: Self Discovery, Researching Family Systems, List Making, Letter Writing and Journaling, Visualizing What You Want, Family Celebrations and Crises, Resolving Inner Conflicts, Preparing for the First Visit Home, and Living From Our Core.

OPTION 1. SELF DISCOVERY

Defining our own patterns of thinking, acting and feeling allows us to stop blaming Mother. We need all the support we can get for this work. Some goals for ourselves might include the following:

- Receiving as well as giving nurturing
- Believing all our feelings are legitimate

- Expanding our concept of mothering to surrogates—neighbours, grandmothers, aunts, teachers.
- Ceasing to demand that Mother make up for all we missed.
- Remembering the "good enough" mothering we have received.

Wendy's Story

My mother modelled our lives on "Father Knows Best." Everything was just so. Our home in a lovely neighbourhood was beautiful and clean. We always had good food and clean clothes. Even our panties were ironed. When Father came home at 6 p.m., three cute, healthy, well-behaved children waited. We said our prayers at night, went to Sunday School, enjoyed pleasant holidays and had many playmates who enjoyed our having the first television on the block. We always did well in school and were encouraged to participate in dancing, music and Brownies. A sense of cooperation filled our home.

My maternal grandmother lived with us. Her Scottish up-and-doing character, a pride of family, and a no-nonsense attitude towards tidy rooms, chores and homework prevailed. We operated under a measure of, "What will the neighbours think?" Knowing what other children suffered, I am grateful for this predictable way of life.

As an adult, however, I knew that something was missing, a deep longing that took years to unfold. Although much care had gone into my upbringing, the sacred layers of emotion and spirit were somehow denied. Feelings were suppressed. I had to behave, submit to parental authority, expect not to be consulted about anything, and not question my parenting. Above all, I was not to have feelings that might threaten my parents' sense of themselves. My job was to be a good girl, try to get it right, and then receive the reward of acknowledgement. Although the body was nourished, well-dressed, bathed and put to bed, the hugs were limited, cool and somewhat perfunctory.

My mum's mood was calm and playful in the early years. Then Grandmother fell ill with a series of strokes and Mother nursed her through to her death. Other family pressures—a move to another city and a hysterectomy—combined to make Mother moody, passively hostile and invariably depressed. Of course, none of this was acknowledged, negotiated or explained. The effect on me was to try harder to please her. Finally, my relationship with my mother could be characterized as emotionally enmeshed and unconscious.

My parents moved to the United States when I was 21. Between my living abroad and my mother moving away, our contact was limited to annual visits, occasional letters, and bi-monthly phone calls. Any chance to gradually move this relationship to a point of increased consciousness or satisfaction was not possible with this sparse schedule. My parents' relationship with one another was primary, and who I was mattered to the level of what they could encompass in their relatively tight framework. The rest was dismissed with silence, superficial concerns and a focus on grand-children.

Problems in my marriage led to therapy and an examination of the longing for connection, approval, and boundary, among other issues. As I worked my way through early wounds and resentments, I gradually became more clear about who I am, from whence I came and what I valued in my life. Eventually, my approach toward my mother became friendly and more attuned to who she was.

OPTION 2. RESEARCHING FAMILY SYSTEMS

Finding intergenerational patterns of beliefs and behaviours can initiate change in relationships. Family maps and genograms make these patterns more visible as well as studying family photo albums and listening to relatives talk about the old days.

Asking the questions no one asks can uncover family secrets. These often explain family behaviours that get passed down from one generation to another. Airing the secrets may release the next generations from inappropriate behaviours. Silence about certain events may have originated to protect the children. Family members can cope with the truth; overprotection for adults is not only unnecessary, it is deadly.

NOTE: Never use a secret to shame, blame or punish a family member. Discretion is needed in this process.

OPTION 3. LIST MAKING

- Take seven sheets of paper and divide each page in half vertically.

- On the left side of one page, write "What I want from Mother." On the right side, write, "What I can give Mother."

What I Want From Mother	What I Can Give Mother
• appreciation	• companionship
• admiration	• sharing my feelings
• no criticism	• comfort
• to be special	• vitality

- Do the same thing on the other six pages, using the following headings:

Daughter's Relationship with Mother

1. What I want from Mother   What I can give Mother
2. What I like about her   What I don't like about her
3. How I am similar to her   How I am different from her
4. What do I value?   What do I want to change?
5. Safe topics to discuss   Unsafe topics
6. Her positive comments   Her negative comments
   to me
7. My positive comments   My negative comments
   to her

OPTION 4. LETTER WRITING AND JOURNALING

- Writing down your feelings can externalize and clarify confused and turbulent emotions. Do not edit or censor them since they may not be mailed.

- Describe a childhood event and feelings associated with it. Tell how it still affects you today. Lastly, say what you want from Mother now. Underline the significant phrases.

- If you decide to mail it, rewrite the letter, perhaps three more times. Between revisions, practice reading it aloud to a friend. If you feel ready, mail it. (Another option is to visit mother and read it aloud to her.)

- To prepare for this, ask two or three people to role play Mother as you read. Ask for their feedback afterward.

Here is such a letter:

Dear Abbie,

I want to talk with you and say some things I've never said before. We've never really talked much about these things. I tried last May to bring them up on the telephone, but you told me not to—to wait until I was next in California. You were right. It's better to discuss these things in person.

I'd like you to listen to me and not interrupt or comment until I've finished. Then you can talk to me. I don't want to get side-tracked from what I consider important. Will you do that?

I think I'm one of the few people who really enjoys my work. This city is a great place for me to live and work, since there's so much happening here. There's no place where I could do this sort of thing as comfortably, because any city with a comparable range of culture would already have people doing what I do. And breaking into the job market would be difficult.

This is my home now, where my friends are, and that's where I expect to stay for the rest of my life. It's unlikely that I'll move back to your city.

That's a kind of external matter, though, and I want to talk to you about me and how I feel. I am comfortable being gay. Though I may have some hang-ups about sex, I don't think they have to do with my sexual orientation. I've had a good 14-year relationship with my lover, but this has changed focus. I want another relationship, and I have to feel more confident about myself before that will happen. I'm still sorting out a lot of hurt and fear about relationships—and there's some anger mixed in there too. I think I have to get over those things before I'm ready to get involved again.

What I'd most like to tell you is that I like my life and I feel responsible for it. I'm not your little girl anymore. I haven't been for years. I'm an adult who can and will make the decisions I want about my life and how to live it. I don't think you've ever treated me as an adult who has that kind of control over what I do. Instead, I feel you see me as an extension of you, someone who has to think, feel and do whatever you think, feel and do. As adults, both of us, we are equals. I'd like you to think of me that way.

Maybe part of the parental way of dealing with children is to be overly protective of them—as a parent would see it, "for the child's own good." But as an adult, I don't want you to treat me that way. I'd like you to try NOT to think of me and speak to me as if I were someone who needed guiding through this world. At least give a thought to what you're about to say to me. Because so much of what you say sounds to me like criticism.

I hear you tell me what to eat, who to relate to, what to wear. I feel controlled and angry by this. Please stop. I know you enjoy giving things to my sister and me. That is one of the ways you show your concern and love for us. What I'd like you to do is offer me something once and then stop. If I accept, fine. I appreciate what you give. If I don't, please don't comment or ask "why not?" And don't push something on me or tell me that I should take it because you say so. I hate that. I get furious with you when you do that. I'm not you! I won't be a carbon copy of you. I'm not your little girl anymore.

Part of this is how I think you handle both my time and my interests. In the past few years, I feel you've been more open about letting me spend my time visiting you as I choose to, instead of organizing that time. I think you still plan some things that involve me without my having a say in the matter. I don't want you to do that. I want to be consulted and asked, not told. Please DON'T tell me that we're having dinner with someone on this day and at this time. Ask me in advance, both if I want to have dinner with that person and whether that time is good for me. Of course, this is a negotiating sort of thing, since we all have independent lives and one person's time might not suit someone else. I don't want any plans made for me without my having a say in it. It's presumptuous of anyone to do so.

It's important for me that you recognize me as an adult. What I've talked about are some of the ways that I feel you haven't done so. I'm still your daughter and you hurt me very much last April by telling me that you were changing your will to leave the bulk of the estate to my sister. I wasn't as upset about the money, as I was hurt because I felt that what you did was to punish me for not being what you wanted me to be. I'm still hurt by that, since it feels like you've cut me off and left me alone. I feel rejected. I feel scared too.

I would like you to offer to give me something freely, because you want to and because you love me. But I want you to do so without conditions. If there are conditions on what you offer, I don't want it.

I want you to recognize me as your daughter, but as your daughter who is grown up and is a responsible adult. I still love you and am conscious of and grateful for everything you've done to help me in my life. But, it's time you see that Jo, the little girl, has become Joanne, the woman who is your equal.

If you want to talk about the things I've said, let's do so. But talk about them with me, not with my sister. These things are between you and me.

Love, Joanne

OPTION 5. VISUALIZING WHAT YOU WANT

Take the list of Mother's negative comments from Option 3. Notice the ones that often lead to arguments.

- With eyes closed, imagine a conversation with Mother. Imagine her as a baseball pitcher and you as a batter.

- See her critical messages as the curve balls she throws at you.

- As the batter, duck these and watch them go by. Refuse to hit them back. Seeing the game for what it is, you can choose not to reply.

- Introduce a safe topic—the weather, a television show, a newspaper item.

- Say goodbye to Mother and slowly come back to the present.

- Taking the initiative alters relationships.

- Practice this exercise until you are ready to try it out with Mother.

OPTION 6. FAMILY CELEBRATIONS AND CRISES

Anniversaries, family reunions, graduations, births, funerals and holidays are significant family rituals. They are also opportunities to observe how we are quickly caught up in childhood patterns and how they are transmitted. These events can be used to experiment with new ways of being that are closer to what we really want instead of tolerating the status quo. Family members may convey the message of "don't do that." Systems resist change. However, since our birthright is to experience pleasure, we can opt for patterns that afford more enjoyment.

Jackie's Celebration

Jackie's parents' wedding anniversary was a week from Tuesday. She, her five brothers and sisters, and their families were expected to attend. It was a command performance she was dreading.

At family gatherings, the men dominated the conversation by talking about financial investments. Forced into silence, the women were bored and resentful. Deciding not to confront the family openly about this, Jackie visualized how she would like to be on that occasion.

Days before the party, she imagined both women and men talking together, playfully recalling earlier days and discussing recent events in their lives. She found herself enjoying this vision.

At the celebration, Jackie arrived with snapshots of a family reunion some years ago. One brother remarked, "We all look bored as hell." A sister commented, "My smile looks like a smirk." The conversation grew lively and energetic with everyone contributing funny stories of family events.

Something different had happened. Although they reverted to talking business after dinner, this had been a crack in the system. Jackie resolved to share her values as a woman more often so she could experience more pleasure in being with her family.

OPTION 7. RESOLVING INNER CONFLICTS

Defense mechanisms are designed to protect against the pain of large or small traumas experienced in childhood. Having our pain seen, heard and comforted by a loved one would have healed the wound. If silence or overt denial surrounds a trauma, we bury it, probably determining never to share it with anyone. We learn not to trust even if there are trustworthy people in our lives later on.

Herein lie our conflicts. When, as adults, we long to feel connected to a trusted other, we unconsciously remain loyal to a powerful former resolution. To risk giving it up means to risk feeling the pain of an earlier wound. Our fear of being overwhelmed, devastated or even annihilated by our pain is as great today as it was in childhood. The conflict is that we long to share, but our fear is too great to allow this.

Since it is fear that keeps us from our longing, can we acknowledge and release this fear which no longer serves as a positive survival mechanism? Can we choose when, with whom and how much to live an open-hearted life?

Resolving inner conflict frees us.

Sarah's Story Continues

Sarah, a woman in her 40s, was feeling buried by her responsibilities of mothering adolescents who were experimenting with life. She was tired of being "the little woman behind her man." She was tired of caring for older, dependent parents. She felt she had no time or permission to care for herself.

"Go home, get busy and forget about yourself!" she was told by a minister. He was exhorting her to do more of what was already wearing her out.

That night she had a dream.

> *I am standing on the east side of my childhood home where I lived when approaching adolescence. It is a gray, misty day. As I look up into the sky, I catch my breath. Small drops of moisture are coagulating to form a rosy pink*

fish that begins swimming in the air. A blue-green fish forms alongside and also swims about.

I begin to call to my husband, "Come see this wonderful thing," but immediately I realize that this is for me.

All her life, Sarah had been called lazy when she was playing "let's pretend." She was labelled selfish if she enjoyed being curious and imaginative, or engaged in day dreaming.

Trying hard to live up to her family's expectations that being unselfish and hard working were a woman's highest values, Sarah felt she had lost her own soul. Her dream brought her face to face with this deep conflict in her life. Like the fish in the sky, she knew how to swim and how to fly when she made time to be amazed, to wonder, and to dream.

Washing her face the morning after her dream, Sarah looked into her own eyes and said, "Welcome home!"

OPTION 8. PREPARING FOR THE FIRST VISIT HOME

Usually we leave home in our 20s to become financially independent. It is in our 30s or 40s that we go back home to leave emotionally. Before beginning this work with our parents, it's a good idea to prepare, plan and rehearse before the first contact. Consider the following:

- If I can't change anyone but myself, and mother may not change, then what do I want from the first visit?

- What is the easiest thing to accomplish?

- What are three small changes that would satisfy me? (One would be sufficient.)

- What can I say or do differently?

- How long can I hold my ground before reverting to old patterns?

- Limit the visit. In advance, state the time of arrival and departure. The goal is to stay an adult and leave before becoming a child again.

- Prepare a list of short sentences using "I" statements to stop the negative patterns. Examples: *I prefer not to discuss that today. I can't talk about that now. I need to change the topic.*

- Resolve to initiate rather than react.

- Take care of myself (see Chapter 7).

Jackie's Story Continues

Here is Jackie's story of her preparation for her first visit home.

Jackie couldn't win any debates with her mother who questioned and criticized her daughter's choices. So, with the help of a friend, she wrote a note to her mother, condensing ten pages into five main points. When she rehearsed it using an audio tape, all she heard was a whisper. The second time she heard a whiny, cranky voice. The third and last time, she heard the calm matter-of-fact voice of a woman. With that attitude, she felt ready to face her mother.

When her mother tried to interrupt her, Jackie simply stated and restated, "Mom, I just want to tell you about myself." To her astonishment, her mother stopped dead in her tracks and said, "Well, you sound pretty sure of yourself today. Perhaps you'd better tell me what's on your mind."

OPTION 9.   LIVING FROM OUR CORE

A major goal in individuation is to defuse the intense feelings we have towards our parents. Releasing energy that has been tied up in these reactive emotions makes it possible to become proactive instead.

The diagram (opposite page) was designed by the late Eva Pierrakos, co-founder with her husband, John, of a body-based therapy called Core Energetics.

It helps clarify the age-old debate about the essential nature of humankind. Seeing the inner spirit of both our mothers and ourselves gives us a larger perspective of the relationship and helps defuse negativity.

After reflecting on this core diagram, we can draw one for ourselves and one for Mother. Placing them side-by-side makes it evident what we need to learn from Mother and what insights we can receive about how to become ourselves.

The Mask (Outer Layer)

This is the outer manifestation of ourselves that we present to the world. How do we want others to see us—caring, competent, warm, tough, firm, decisive?

These are all qualities of our social mask which are expressed either in pleasing or rebellious behaviours. At its worst, our mask keeps us performing, trying hard to meet others' expectations. At its best, it makes life easier, more efficient, more pleasant. Either way, we feel something important is missing. Life tends to be meaningless and unfulfilling.

The Lower Self (Negativity Layer)

This is the part of us that others usually find irritating and unacceptable. Family, friends, church and society say, "Don't be like that."

Some of the feelings that characterize this layer are: criticism, contempt, arrogance, jealousy, self-pity, whining and

The Core Diagram

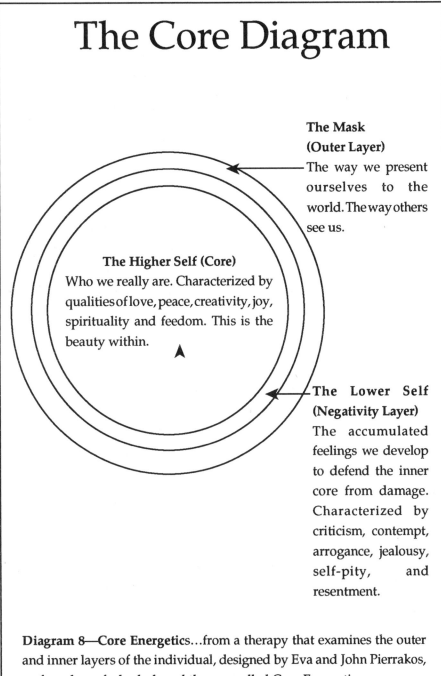

**The Mask
(Outer Layer)**
The way we present ourselves to the world. The way others see us.

The Higher Self (Core)
Who we really are. Characterized by qualities of love, peace, creativity, joy, spirituality and feedom. This is the beauty within.

**The Lower Self
(Negativity Layer)**
The accumulated feelings we develop to defend the inner core from damage. Characterized by criticism, contempt, arrogance, jealousy, self-pity, and resentment.

Diagram 8—Core Energetics...from a therapy that examines the outer and inner layers of the individual, designed by Eva and John Pierrakos, co-founders of a body-based therapy called Core Energetics.

resentment. It is from this place that we blame or shame others—or ourselves.

Subtle and blatant manipulation, control and acts of verbal, physical or sexual abuse, are negativity at its worst.

Protecting and defending our core from damage or violence is the best feature. As adults we can be more flexible in choosing when to be more, or less, defensive in our relationships.

The Higher Self (The Core)

When we ask, "Who am I?" we are expressing a longing to live more from our core, to know the deeper parts of ourselves that have been denied, repressed and forgotten. When we ask, "What do I want most in life?" the answers are probably core qualities—like peace, creativity, joy, spirituality and freedom.

One fairy tale tells about a princess losing her golden ball. The princess can only recover her ball by accepting help from a disgusting frog. The frog is insistent that she treat him as an equal.

The golden ball is a symbol of our golden core and the frog might be synonymous with the lower self. The princess doesn't want to have anything to do with the frog, but realizes she can't regain her golden ball without his help. When she agrees to respect him, allowing him to eat from her plate, sleep on her pillow and (ugh!) even kiss her, the frog turns into a prince.

This is a story of transformation, of reclaiming all the parts of herself, living from her core rather than her mask.

Both daughters and mothers can choose to do this work of transformation. Different situations present themselves for our work—difficulties with a boss, mate, major life change or loss. One that carries the most emotional energy is the relationship with Mother. Whether alive or dead, she is one of the best avenues for our individuation process.

GUIDELINES

- Draw a core diagram for yourself, and another one for Mother. Size the circles as you perceive them. How large is the outer layer compared to the inner core?

- Place them side-by-side. How do they fit? How does one compare with the other?

- Spend some time reflecting on these two diagrams to find out what can be learned.

- Use the following diagram to list the adjectives that apply to you.

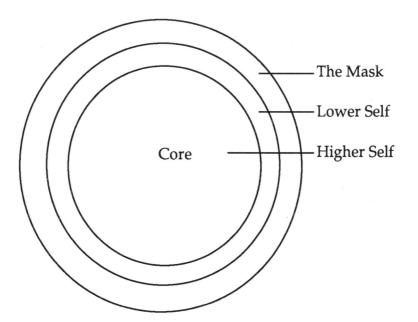

HIGHLIGHTS

- Planning and researching is essential to a first successful reconnection with Mother.

- Start with simple, small steps. Become the initiator of change rather than the reactor.

- Practice one-liners that stop the negative patterns.

- Understand "good-enough mothering" and stop demanding that Mother change.

- Responsibility for change rests with Daughter.

- This work is for our own development.

- As children we protect our core being with defenses that need to be addressed as adults. An outer social mask and a layer of negativity protect our core.

- It is essential to love and nurture ourselves.

THE NINE MAJOR OPTIONS
Option 1.   Self Discovery
Option 2.   Researching Family Systems
Option 3.   List Making
Option 4.   Letter Writing and Journaling
Option 5.   Visualizing what you want
Option 6.   Family Celebrations and Crises
Option 7.   Resolving Inner Conflicts
Option 8.   Preparing for the First Visit Home
Option 9.   Living From Our Core

CHAPTER 11

When Persephone descended into the underworld she made the shift from being mothered to mothering herself and others. When she emerged into the upper world again, she was no longer a little girl, but a woman equal in power to Demeter.

11

GOODBYE MOTHER

When change comes, there is a goodbye waiting to happen. Since long-term relationships need renewal from time to time, refusal to say goodbye to the old prevents us from beginning anew. Seldom are we prepared to say goodbye.

There is a strong universal belief that a mother is a mother all her life and a daughter is daughter. This is an illusion. As adult daughters we can choose to relinquish the roles that gave our lives meaning while growing up. We can also release Mother from the job of parenting us and become our own mother.

"You can always depend on Helen; she's such a good girl," "You can never depend on Laura, she's so selfish," or "Janice is such a joker you can never take her seriously." These are the messages we've grown up with. The list of such identifying labels is endless and damaging. Saying goodbye means letting go of them. It also means saying goodbye to the role Mother assumed during the mothering years. Until we see Mother as a person, we are still caught expecting her to mother us.

On the next pages women describe making that shift from being mothered to mothering themselves. They each say goodbye to their mothers in their own way.

MONICA'S STORY

Monica, a typical dutiful daughter, writes the following letter.

Dear Mother,

The women in our family really learned subservience—as have I! I know I'll never have the kind of relationship I really want if I don't get over this...subservience, for want of a better word.

The problem in the failure of my first marriage was that I felt I had no rights. All these years I know you've gone on the assumption that you had no rights. God knows you've supported everyone else. I've really tried to follow in your footsteps, but I ache from the pain of no time for myself to live up to my own potential. I feel so ashamed of how boring, complaining and old I am. I'm desperate to change, to find that old self who had hope and vitality—but I'm finding it damn hard. You have been an inspiration in so many ways...and now I need to be alone to make a life of my own.

One of the ways to individuate is to go back home again to ask the *terrible* questions, or make the statements we've never dared say before. Monica told her mother, "When I say no to Dad, you tell me you 'can't take it any more,' and that all this fighting means you have to listen to his tirades and your blood pressure is already high, and would I please do whatever it is he wants. I give in, say yes, and live to regret it."

After five years of bad Pap tests, Monica was afraid that cancer was the price she would have to pay for following her mother's "peace at any price" lifestyle. "I'm tired of Dad making decisions for me," Monica tells her mother. "I just won't allow it. It's one thing to say that to him, it's much harder to say it to you. I feel bad about abandoning you. I just can't be there for you. I want my own life."

Going home to cut our emotional umbilical cords after age

30 frees us. Rituals and retirement parties to honour moms can create appropriate boundaries. Boundaries are things like: making the time and space to do the things that feel nurturing to us, defining the limits of our involvement with the people around us, especially family. The relationship with mother may become one of friendship. If that is not possible, at least we can function woman to woman. Equalizing the power between us is an important focus of this stage of life.

It helps to create a ritual to acknowledge this event: writing a letter, taking Mother to dinner for a face-to-face talk. These are the moments when we tell her who we are and what we want in the relationship now. Underneath the words is a meaning that may sound like this:

"When I was little, you were big. I was helpless and you were in charge, keeping me safe. I'm not your little girl anymore. I'm my own mother now. I'm learning to nurture myself. So, Mom, I'm letting you off the hook."

Sue's Story
Sue, an independent woman in the world of business, wrote but never mailed the following letter to prepare herself for a talk with her mother over dinner.

Dear Mother,

I want to tell you that I'm gay—I feel like I lived a lie most of my adult life. I want to share not only the pain of pretending, but also some of the joy of not having to pretend any more—the joy of being in a warm, loving relationship—the very thing most parents would be delighted to hear about their adult children. But I'm not sure what your reaction will be.

If I continue to protect you from your pain, mine increases. I deny myself and all that is important to me. I'm afraid of really hurting you. I'm stuck in your pain.

When I listen to you, I hear a message of reproach: I should be doing more; I should fix it all. Well, Mom, I protest! I can't fix it. I can't make you feel safe.

You do not know who I am and I would like you to accept some responsibility for not knowing. I have my own life and my own pain with which I must struggle—and from which I will learn and grow. I don't need you to fix it or make it better. I don't need your protection.

I need you to know me a little better and to accept the part of me I wish to share.

"Don't hurt your mother" was a strong message in Sue's family. Peggy, her mother, looked pale and depressed. She often threatened suicide when Sue was growing up. Survival for little Sue meant being loyal to the family. Now she is faced with the dilemma: "Am I going to continue to live for Mom, or do I save my own life?"

Sue feared that telling her mother she was gay would shock, upset and hurt her. Maybe it would be "the last straw that broke her mother's back." Would mom say, "This will kill me," or "You'll be the death of me"?

"Can I stand to face the consequences?" Sue asked her therapist. "What if she dies? Can I live with my guilt?"

"Whoa!" exclaimed the therapist. "Those are global leaps you're taking. You don't have that kind of power over her life or her death. A bigger question here is: how much more of your mother's pain and your own pain can you take?"

"Not much." Sue answered.

"So what do you need to do to save your own life?" inquired her therapist.

For better or worse, since homosexuality was at the center of her being, Sue wanted to share this secret with her mother. Perhaps this would change the relationship from boring and draining to lively and full of juice.

Knowing that Peggy usually grabbed the limelight with a long litany of suffering, Sue planned a way to stay centered.

First, calling her mother *Peggy* would set the stage for a different way to talk—more adult to adult. Next Sue asked to meet at a neutral place instead of Mom's home. She wanted to change the pattern of Peggy talking and Sue listening.

Sitting on a park bench, Sue announced, "Peggy, I have some important things I want to say to you. I'd appreciate it if you would listen for 10 minutes without talking, and afterwards you'll have all the time you want."

"Of course dear," Peggy's wide blue eyes looked startled. "Haven't I always been here when you needed to talk?" Sue recognized that Peggy was trying to shift the focus to herself while implying criticism of her daughter. "How could Sue see her as anything but a dedicated mother?" was reflected in the question, along with "How could you talk to your mother this way?"

Sue repeated her question, "Does that mean it's okay for me to take 10 minutes?"

"Yes dear," her mother replied. "I'll do my best to be quiet."

Sue told Peggy about when she first knew she was gay, and how she had always protected her mother by keeping it secret. Not having her mother as a confidante hurt Sue. It was hard to mother her mother and not feel mothered herself. Trying to figure out how to fix things for Mom had given her migraine headaches when she was 10. Sue continued, "I'm still stuck in your pain, and that increases my pain. All I want is for you to accept who I am, and who I am is gay."

Sue's mother did not die on the spot as Sue had feared. Instead her responses were more concerned with her own adequacy: "I always did the best I could, what did I do wrong to have you turn out this way?" Since it was now Peggy's turn to talk, Sue bit her tongue and listened as she'd promised. After eight minutes Peggy subtly shifted from self pity to curiosity.

"I've always wondered what it would be like to make love to another woman," she commented self-consciously. "What is it like?"

Slowly Sue and Peggy continued to open up their relationship. This doesn't always happen. One daughter who had accepted an exciting career advancement across the country was countered with her mother's blackmail, "I'll die if you leave me." Her daughter left and the mother died three months later. Although this was a horrible goodbye, the daughter realized that she had broken her mother's iron-fisted control at last. She had chosen her own life over her mother's life. Saving her own was possible; saving her mother's was impossible. Each of us is responsible for choosing to live or to die.

Following family rules, roles, beliefs and behaviours and forgetting who we are, is like being under a spell. As adults we have to wake up, to become aware again of ourselves. Making choices for our lives means breaking the spell.

Fairy tales tell us truths about our human existence. They tell about powerful spells and how to break them. Breaking them is dedicated, long term work, and we're worth the time and energy it takes. Fairy tales tell us we need help; it's usually a fairy godmother who comes to the princess' rescue. A fairy godmother has more power than ordinary people. We receive this super power from people who want the best for themselves and us—a grandmother or grandfather, a best friend, a therapist, a caring group. The Japanese Buddhists have a saying: you have to do it alone, but you don't have to do it by yourself.

Joan's Story Continues

Joan wanted a better relationship with her mother. She could never remember being a child. Joan came for a few therapy sessions with her youthful looking 70-year-old mother, Agnes. Joan hoped Agnes would hear the pain she'd suffered from never having been a child.

What I sought was for my mother to finally see me as a child, to recognize the loss I felt around both childhoodlessness and childlessness.

I've often felt I was the last of a long line of women who didn't want to be mothers, but I never thought I was the end of a long line of women who simply hadn't learned to be good mothers.

Mother and I came away from the first session elated. For me, the greatest relief was to realize, and to have my mother realize, that I wasn't the person responsible for her lack of self-confidence and the pain in her life. The lid had been opened on her childhood pain that she had so carefully suppressed all her life. That became part of re-creating authenticity in our relationship.

Joan was beginning to see her mother as not only lacking in nurturing abilities but as another woman who, like herself, had not been nurtured. This was a major leap in equalizing the power between them. Agnes, the mother, had given too much of her power to Joan, her daughter.

Now it was openly acknowledged between the two that Agnes' lack of confidence had stemmed from her own childhood deprivation, not because Joan was more competent than her mother. It was clear that mother's work was to take responsibility for her own pain, and that Joan's was to stop taking responsibility for Mother.

Whether these two will find enough common ground as equal adults is the risk they now face. Can they be authentic enough together to form a friendship based on interdependence?

"Until we see our mother as a woman, we see every woman as our mother," goes the old saying. Our friendships with other women, including our daughters, are shaped from our perspectives of our mothers. All relationships are limited by hopes that we will at last receive the nurturing we never got from Mother.

Monica's Story Continues

The most important part of these "Goodbye Mother" dialogues is to convey what we want in the relationship now. Monica tells Mom in her letter:

> *I really appreciate that we haven't been having as much phone contact. I need more space if I'm to succeed at a career. Rather than shooting the breeze, I'd like more quality time with you. While I know you love me, I'd like more encouragement from you as a person, another woman.*
>
> *You are great, and I love you.*

A letter like Monica's creates visible evidence of equality. It is a way to ritualize the end of Mother seeing Daughter as her little girl and of Daughter allowing herself to be Mother's little girl.

This is a goodbye of great magnitude. While we will still continue to mother loved ones and be mothered ourselves, this is a crucial time in mid-life—when we claim self responsibility. In the words of one daughter:

> *What I'd like most to tell you is that I like my life and I feel responsible for it. I'm not your little girl any more, and I haven't been for years. I am an adult, and can and will make the decisions about my life and how I live it. I don't think you've ever treated me as an adult who has that kind of control over what she does. Instead, I feel you see me as an extension of you, someone who has to think, feel and do whatever you think, feel and do. As adults, both of us are equals, and I'd like you to think of me that way.*
>
> *I still love you. I'm conscious of and grateful for everything you've done to help me in my life. It's time to acknowledge that your little girl has become a woman who is your equal.*

GUIDELINES

Writing

Write a letter to your mother.

- Recall a childhood incident you want to discuss with her.
- What did you feel about it then? How does it keep you stuck today?
- How would you like your relationship to change today?
- What are you willing to do or not willing to do?
- Read your letter aloud to two or three good friends.
- Revise it several times, if necessary, until it says exactly what you want to say.

Talking

Talk face-to-face to your mother.

- Call her by her first name (this defines a new boundary and declares a change in the relationship).
- Agree to a time and length of time. Find a neutral place (not Mom's turf).
- Ask for 10 minutes without interruption.
- Tell her she'll have all the time she wants to talk afterwards and you'll listen.
- Remember, having the courage to do this *is* success, no matter how she responds!

HIGHLIGHTS

- Stop being loyal to mother. Start being loyal to yourself. Tell your own truth.

- Say out loud to Mother what you could never say as a child. Disclose family secrets. Ask the terrible questions you were never supposed to ask.

- Tell Mother what kind of relationship you want now.

- Be specific: phone before you visit; ask rather than demand; don't comment on weight or hairstyle; give positive comments instead of criticism.

CHAPTER 12

Persephone's decision to leave home created unfinished business between both women. They needed time to free themselves from old roles. Becoming equals allowed them to connect as one woman to another.

12

HELLO
WOMAN

Saying goodbye erases labels—the dutiful one, the rebellious one, the smart one, the stupid one, the beautiful one, the ugly one. We can choose how we want to reconnect with Mother. These choices are varied: we may be friends, we may not like each other but remain distantly connected, or if the relationship is too toxic we may choose to withdraw, not out of revenge, but from our need to protect ourselves. Saying hello means to see Mother as another woman—an equal. This can change other relationships too.

Here women tell us how their relationships changed and continue to change—for better or for worse!

BERNICE'S STORY
In her family of origin, Bernice felt like the ugly duckling, the dumb one, the scapegoat. Roles of the smart one and the beautiful one were already taken by older sisters. Someone needed to carry the opposites in order to bring balance to the family system. So Bernice dutifully complied. Some years later she declared in a letter her resignation from this role:

Dear Mother:

I am going through a very introspective time in my life—trying to figure out who I am—apart from being your daughter, a wife and a mother of three. I have invested so much time in trying to be what everyone else expected that I lost much of "me" along the way. I never developed, or grew, and as a result, I have been a very scared and dependent person all my life. Now I'm finally learning to trust myself, accept myself, and even love myself. I feel like a small child taking her first steps. It's all very frightening but promising too.

This letter is a declaration of my independence. I am not trying to change you or even punish you, but rather I'm telling you that I am an adult and expect to be treated with the same respect as any other adult, and that at long last, I have cut my own umbilical cord!

The key to our individuation is no longer needing to see Mother in her role of mother, but as a person with whom we are equal in our womanhood. Then we can remember the old relationship and create a new bond based on equality.

Cutting the emotional umbilical cord does not mean being completely independent. It means claiming the choice of when to be independent and when to be dependent. Interdependence is the freedom to choose. Cutting the cord means to free ourselves from the roles we played in our families as we grew up—roles that may keep us feeling unsatisfied in our relationships today. Often we still believe that our roles define who we are in the world.

As human beings we carry within us our best and our worst, the bright and the dark sides of ourselves. In most families these qualities become personified in individuals—the golden girl or the black sheep roles. When we are children, roles can provide a stable system in which to grow up. As adults we may challenge these limitations, expanding our potential for wholeness.

A crisis in the family provides an excellent opportunity to initiate change. Usually crises are viewed as disasters happening to us. In retrospect we may feel they were blessings in disguise, opportunities to be individuals in our families of origin, not just in our roles as the smart one or the dumb one.

For two long years, a cold war had been carried on in Bernice's family. While the adults barely spoke, the ones who suffered the most were the three grandchildren. Two years were an eternity to them.

Feeling like an inadequate daughter, Bernice was very fearful of confronting a critical mother and an over-achieving father. Out of her despair, she realized she had to take a stand for herself.

Bernice's letter instigated the break-up of the deep freeze and challenged everyone's position at the same time. Until now, Mother had been the family's switchboard operator—all interactions were processed through her. Dad's favourite one-liner had been, "Speak to your mother." This time, however, he wrote Bernice a long warm letter telling his story of how the cold war began, how he hated it, how he wished it would end. He expressed his love for his daughter, son-in-law and grandchildren.

Mom sent Bernice a critical, even vitriolic, response. Once on her own path, however, Bernice didn't waver or crumble. In the therapy room, she confessed, "I love my mother, but I don't know if I can ever like her."

The ripples created by her letter kept reverberating. A large family celebration was coming up, offering a great way for Bernice's family to meet with the grandparents for the first time in two years. Intense feelings could be defused in a safe environment.

Bernice's original goal in therapy was to achieve a reunion of the two families. Now she discovered that she had changed in the process and was considering other options. Realizing she had been too enmeshed in her relationships with family members, she studied her own motives more carefully. She repeatedly asked herself, "What do I want, even if it displeases my parents?" She learned to protect herself from much of Mom's criticism by limiting the length of their conversations, by meeting either on Bernice's turf or on neutral ground, and by engaging in safe topics—the weather or the grandchildren.

Bernice felt ready to invite her parents for a week-end. It turned out to be a pleasant event. At one point, she and her mother happened to be in Bernice's bedroom. "I'm glad these last two years are behind us, Bernice," Mother began. "You and your family have had enough trouble to last a lifetime."

"I always felt guilty for our problems," Bernice replied. "I thought we should be like you and Dad. You always seemed to get along so well."

"Well, we are enjoying each other right now," Mom said, "but we've had our hard times too, you know."

"No, I didn't know." Bernice was silent, but Mom had revealed as much as she could. Still it was a first foray into becoming equals, perhaps possible friends. Instead of the usual critical parent/inadequate daughter dialogue, it was a peer-to-peer exchange.

Bernice presents a snapshot of the growth process she was fully engaged in for two years:

> *I am learning to grieve for the little girl in me who felt that she owed her life to those around her. I tried so hard to be a carbon copy of Mum. I thought it would make me more lovable and acceptable. But I'm not like Mum. I am Me—apart from being anyone's daughter, wife or mother—whoever Me is! It's as if I stopped developing emotionally at three years of age. Growing up after 30 is not easy. Learning to love myself has proven even more difficult. And it's nothing that anyone can do for me. I am slowly beginning to see the light at the end of the tunnel.*

On Equal Terms—Sue and Peggy

Earlier we saw how Sue risked sharing her lesbian orientation with Peggy, her mother. At first Mother responded with the expected, "I guess I wasn't a very good mother," and "what did I do wrong that you turned out this way?" She was looking for comfort and reassurance from her daughter, a trademark of the relationship as it had been. When Sue didn't respond, but sat silently, Peggy tentatively disclosed a little of her dissatisfaction with her own sex life and her lack of sexual feelings in it.

This may not have been the response Sue hoped for, but when a daughter and mother begin sharing some of their sex lives, it is an equalizing of the power in the relationship.

> **Note:** It is usually inappropriate for a mother to initiate this kind of disclosure with a daughter who is under the age of 30. A daughter may ask for information about sex but doesn't want to know about her mother's sexual experiences. Daughters do not yet know who they are. They need to establish themselves in some way—a career, a circle of friends, hobbies, interests, perhaps marriage and children. Often daughters are in their 40s when they begin this work with their mothers.

Disclosure is high risk work since daughters can never know how their mothers will respond—with a tirade or by opening up. So daughters do this for themselves, not for the responses from mothers. It's heroic work, like open-heart surgery without the anaesthetic!

Sometime later when Sue and Peggy met for lunch, Peggy confided, "You know, your father always came too soon for me. I've wondered for years if making love would be better with a woman. Maybe if I'd been born in this day and age, I'd be a lesbian."

Sue realized her mother was a pretty neat woman. A few days later, she wrote a note to tell Peggy how she felt:

It has just occurred to me how much I like you. I love you, but I also like you. As I ponder this thought, there is a warmth flowing through me. Recalling memories has brought back many good thoughts and feelings, and a number of these are shared times with you.

Joan's Story Continues

Joan has no memories of being a child, only a capable grownup. The daughter and mother relationship was reversed in her family. Daughter Joan was the capable one and her mother, Agnes, was the inadequate. In a therapy session, Joan told her mother that she had never felt mothered by her. Eyes widened in surprise, Agnes blurted out, "But I didn't know how."

Agnes continued to talk about how it had seemed more important for her mother to spend time with her father than with her. Agnes began to realize she had never felt mothered either. Feeling the loss, she began to cry. Joan immediately leaped for the tissue box before the therapist could lift a hand—a pattern of caring for her mother learned in childhood. Agnes had never resolved her pain with her mother; consequently she laid it unconsciously on her daughter's *little adult* shoulders. Out of this common deprivation, Joan and Agnes cried on each other's shoulders—not as a daughter and mother, but as two women with the same pain.

Later Joan reflected:

The most telling thing is that I began to sleep well. For more than 10 years—maybe 15—I've been taking something to get to sleep.

Since Agnes always denied she had any problems in her life, we now focus on Agnes' losses—recent unmourned deaths, and long past childhood wounds. This is an authenticity that is wonderful. We are out of the communication box we were in."

Some of the pain has dropped from Joan's shoulders.

Deborah's Story Continues

Deborah writes about the shift in her relationship with her parents:

> *I am letting go of Mother's stance that life is too hard for her. This has always prevented me from getting my own needs met. Dad and Mom were both present one day when I became angry about Mom trying to control every little thing. We all said what we had to say, cried together, and then laughed together.*

> *Later Dad took me aside and said, "Your mother has a heavy load to carry. You shouldn't hurt her like that."*

> *I replied, "Dad, you can be angry and that's okay. Mom can be angry and that's okay. It's time I can be angry and have it be okay." Dad nodded his head in agreement and patted me on the shoulder.*

> *I felt they now had both seen me as a grownup for the first time.*

Speaking her mind brought into sharp relief that the function of the triangle—Mom, Dad, and Deborah—was to protect Mom. Father took Deborah aside, instructing her not to hurt her mother. The message really was: "Don't change." As a child Deborah had no choice but to follow the family rules. As an adult she recognizes how they prevented her from getting her own needs met, so she has changed the rules.

Here's what followed this confrontation:

> *I have gone through a period of letting in my mom's new eagerness to nurture me. Since I shared my hurt, she wants to "make up" for what I perceived was lacking. The pleasurable part is that it feels sincere. As I was leaving one day, Mom said, "It was a pleasure to have you." This was a first and it felt very peer-like.*

Change and growth may have chameleon-like qualities. We can change in an instant, though it's more likely to take place gradually over years. Sometimes a person opens up once, but then closes down again.

For Daughter to change within herself and then allow Mother to see and hear this change is a major transformation.

The stories in this book have no ending; they are always going on, even after death. A mother may still be alive although she *died* emotionally years ago. Another may already be dead, but she will always be alive and vibrant for her daughter.

Bernadette—A Daughter and Mother In-Between

The following is written by a family therapist who is both a daughter and a mother. As Bernadette wrestles with the spectre of asking her daughter Paige to leave the family home, she writes poignantly of her feelings about separation and she recalls memories of her own separation from her mother.

> *From the moment I was pregnant, I knew that the precious life within me was a temporary gift, a loan to embrace, treasure, cultivate and enjoy in my home for a very limited time. When I recognized this, however, I never envisioned how the giving up of the treasure would occur—the accepting of my child as an adult woman.*

> *Complicating my dilemma is my recent struggle to forego ideas regarding what I believe is best from the perspective of a woman in her 50s. In relinquishing the treasure, I have had to respect my daughter's choices—the choices of a 22-year-old—when they don't conform to choices I would have her make.*

> *My delightful, intelligent, sensitive daughter has decided to work for a year before entering graduate school in another city. She wants to do this while living at home where, as I see it, she could enjoy the ambiguous world of half-child, half-adult. I feel an agonizing fear that this emerging adult will not care for the treasure I have given her. As a marriage and family therapist, I*

know that the longer one holds and nurtures a treasure, the more difficult it becomes to let go.

In that light, I am surprised when I entertain the thought that she must find her own living arrangements. Both my husband and I fear Paige will view our decision as abandonment rather than our faith in her capacity to experience her own strength. I view the move as handing over my treasure to my daughter.

Believing that each child needs to care for and support herself, I sense my daughter's reluctance to leave is the fear of the unknown world outside along with the ready comfort of home. I recall my own fear at leaving home. My parents expected I would remain at home until I married and were horrified when I chose at age 24 to live with a female friend and complete graduate school on my own. However, I now realize how much I tried to delay the process of leaving—nearly failing chemistry in my senior year in high school; nearly failing a required course in my senior year at university; and taking a very long time to complete papers for my advanced graduate work.

While I view Paige's staying at home as my own failure, my mother viewed my leaving as her failure. She believed in women having ongoing support, leaving home only to marry and carry over the love, emotional and financial support of the childhood home. When I chose to establish myself with my own lifestyle and distinctive surroundings, Mother felt she had failed me.

Now, at this moment, I feel enormous loss at the thought of my daughter living apart. I delight in our talks and shared professional interests. We attend conferences together, then compare notes and ideas. We share a close bond which I hope will continue when we live separately, but I fear it may be broken.

The letting go has been gradual over the years. While I am pleased that my children can cook for themselves, launder their clothes and keep house, I discover the need to accept their different styles of neatness. I am learning to modify my ways and respect theirs. I am reminded of how difficult their first overnight camping trip was for them and for me, and how they came to relish the overnight summer camp as I relished the quiet of the house. While I know how children grow from such experience, I retain my own fears.

My role with Paige has evolved from one of caretaker, protector, safety-rules setter, guide and ongoing supporter to the role of resource person with intermittent support provided as requested. Ours is a very special friendship.

At the same time I wrestle with releasing Paige from the daughter-mother relationship, I am also releasing my mother. I am releasing my mother from the perspective of my hurting-child part so that I can appreciate the enormous difficulty she had in raising a daughter who didn't always act in ways she thought best. I have come to appreciate my mother as a person who gave what she could in spite of her own hurts from her own growing up years. I can now see her as a remarkably strong, extremely intelligent woman who conveyed to me an intense belief in my abilities, a woman who has always been a support through the most adverse times.

I hope my daughter will come to see me with the same understanding. Because my daughter is strong and has so much integrity, I believe she will manage, either because of my actions or in spite of them. In writing this piece, I am reminded of Paige's myriad beautiful qualities that will enable her to fulfill her gifts, care for herself and continue her loving ties, not only with me but also with others in her family.

This period has helped me to distinguish between abandonment and setting loved ones free to establish their own ways. It has reminded me that separation does not equate with disconnection. Those I love are always with me and I with them.

Like my mother, as long as I live, I too will be there for my daughter as she needs me. But now, I also know she will be there for me.

In learning to accept the choices our mothers made for their lives, we begin to free up our own life energy. Rather than unconsciously following in our mothers' footsteps, we can create what we want. Life is like a tapestry—we weave our own individual threads into patterns of who we are becoming.

The work does not end with saying goodbye to Mother in her role and greeting her as a woman. The relationship may not change once and for all. Traces of ingrained patterns linger. Deeply embedded habits may not be totally removed.

We know the hard work is done when we can face the past, establish ground rules for a new relationship, and look toward the future expectantly. The gift every daughter can receive from this work with her mother is the gift of focus—on who we are, where we came from and where we're going.

Hello, Woman!

GUIDELINES

Reflecting

Develop one-liners for encounters with Mother to help you stay centered:

- *Have you got 10 minutes to listen?*
- *I have something important I want to say.*
- *I want to be free to make my own choices.*
- *I have to go now.*
- *I can't hear any more.*
- *I have only 15 minutes.*
- *I'm not your little girl any more.*
- *I'm the expert on me.*

Visualizing—Gift-Giving

- Find a time and place to focus on yourself. Be comfortable, close your eyes and breathe deeply for a while. Choose a place in your mind's eye for this imagery to happen.

- Now set the stage: What time of year is it? What kind of day is it? What time of day? Inside or outside? Take time to see, hear, smell and feel your surroundings in specific detail.

- Now place mother in this environment. Is she standing, sitting or lying? What is she wearing? Notice the colour of her hair.

- Look into her eyes and ask her for something both visible and tangible that symbolizes her power with you. See her giving it to you. See yourself receiving it. Be aware of how you feel. You may not be ready to visualize this gift yet. Perhaps you have more important work to do first.

- When you feel ready, visualize a tangible gift, that you can hold in your hand, that symbolizes your power with your mother. See yourself giving it to her. See her accepting it. Be with your feelings.

- Take your time, come back to the room, stretch, open your eyes. Draw and colour a picture of the gifts you visualized.

- When you feel ready, ask your mother to do this imagery. Compare your imagery with hers, if you both choose.

Cherish these images as valuable gifts.

HIGHLIGHTS

- Childhood family roles and rules provided stability. As adults they prevent us from getting our own needs met.

- A crisis provides the opportunity for change.

- Writing a letter of what we felt, where we are now, and what we want, is one way to initiate change.

- The message we are likely to receive: "Don't change."

- Changes are made consciously. Tell Mother what hurts, betrays, negates, as well as what is nurturing.

- Be aware of old patterns when they happen, and extricate ourselves. Stay centered. Stand our ground. Know our limits.

- Contact our worst fears, our greatest hopes: accept that reality is somewhere in between.

- Transitions, like saying goodbye and hello, are uncomfortable and painful. Even if we don't like it, we may choose to stay with the familiar.

- The lifelong task of a daughter is to "mother" herself.

- Wouldn't it be great if both daughters and mothers could share their "heroine's journey" in life?

The Thread Goes On

We look backward
    To our mothers who gave us birth,
    To their mothers…and all the mothers before them.

As we reweave anew these tangled threads,
We look forward
    To the birth of our daughters' dreams
    As they reweave ours.

GLOSSARY

boundaries	setting appropriate limits for ourselves and conveying these to appropriate others
disengaged	distant
enmeshed	overinvolved
family map	a diagram of our childhood family system
family of origin	our childhood family
genogram	drawing an expanded family map which includes three or more generations
isomorphism	transferring our family system to everyone we meet
individuation	taking full responsibility for becoming who we are; making the shift from being mothered to mothering ourselves
nuclear family	our present family
triangulation	a relationship shared by three people
visualization	a picture in our mind's eye

RESOURCE BOOKS

Arcana, Judith, *Our Mother's Daughters,* Shameless Hussy Press, 1979

Baldwin, Christina, *One To One, Self Understanding Through Journal Writing,* M. Evans and Co., 1977

Bardwick, Judith, *Readings on the Psychology of Women,* Harper & Row, 1972

Bassoff, Evelyn, *Mothers and Daughters: Loving and Letting Go,* NAL Books, 1988

Bernard, Jessie, *The Future of Motherhood,* The Dial Press, 1974

Caplan, Paula, *Don't Blame Mother,* HarperCollins, 1989

_____ *Between Women: Lowering the Barriers,* Spectrum Publications, 1981

Chernin, Kim, *In My Mother's House* , Ticknor and Fields, 1983

Chesler, Phyllis, *With Child,* Avon Books, 1978

Chodorow, Nancy, *The Reproduction of Mothering,* University of California, 1978

Debold, Elizabeth, Wilson, Marie, and Malave, Ioelisse, *Mother Daughter Revolution,* Addison Wesley Press, 1993

Edelman, Hope, *Motherless Daughters: The Legacy of Loss,* Addison-Wesley, Canada, 1994

Eichenbaum, Louise, and Orbach, Susie, *What Do Women Want* , Coward-McCann, 1983

Friday, Nancy, *My Mother, My Self,* Delacorte Press, 1977

Gilbert, Lucy, and Webster, Paula, *Bound By Love—The Sweet Trap of Daughterhood,* Beacon Press, 1982

Hammer, Signe, *Mothers and Daughters,* New American Library of Canada, Scarborough, 1976

Hall, Nor, *The Moon and the Virgin,* Harper & Row, 1980

Herman, Nini, *Too Long a Child: The Mother-Daughter Dyad,* Free Association Books, 1989

Howard, Jane, *A Different Woman,* Avon Books, 1973

Kirsten, Grace and Robertielle, Robert, *Big You, Little You,* The Dial Press, 1975

Lowinsky, Naomi Ruth, *The Motherline*, Tarcher/Perigee, 1992

Merriam, Eve, *Growing Up Female in America: Ten Lives*, Dell Publishing Co., 1961

Miller, Alice, *Thou Shalt Not Be Aware*, Meridian Press, 1986

Olson, T., *Mothers to Daughters, Daughters to Mothers*, The Feminist Press, 1984

Payne, Karen, editor, *Between Ourselves: Letters Between Mothers and Daughters*, Houghton Mifflin Co., 1983

Rich, Adrienne, *Of Woman Born, Motherhood as Experience and Institution*, Bantam Books, 1976

Rothamn, Sheila M., *Women's Proper Place*, Basic Books, Inc., 1978

Secunda, Victoria, *When You and Your Mother Can't Be Friends*, Dell Press, 1990

Shain, Merle, *Hearts That We Broke Long Ago*, McClelland & Stewart, 1983

Spretnak, Charlene, *Lost Goddesses of Early Greece*, Beacon Press, 1978

Walters, Carter, Papp and Silverstein, *The Invisible Web*, Guilford Press, 1988

ABOUT THE AUTHORS

Mary Dell

One of ten children, Mary's mother, Edith, fostered an ongoing interest in family history which later resulted in Mary's studies in family systems. Out of this grew her work in daughter mother relationships as one of the most effective ways women as daughters can achieve our own personhood.

After raising four daughters, Mary began studies as a psychotherapist, receiving a Master's Degree in Marriage, Family and Child Therapy. At this time she also earned a diploma in Bioenergetic Analysis. Mary's daughters are Elizabeth, Christina, Cynthia and Lorraine.

She has been in private practice in Toronto since 1973. Recently she completed extensive renovation on a barn at her country home where she now offers creative therapy workshops at "The Driveshed Retreat."

Mary's daughter, Christina, recently told her, "Seeing you fulfill your dreams makes me realize I can too."

Marilyn Irwin Boynton

Marilyn credits her own joyful and painful life experiences and those of her clients for the inspiration to write this book. In mid-life, Marilyn was able to reweave a satisfying relationship with her own mother, Beatrice, before her death at age 90.

Boynton is a Registered Nurse who earned a Masters Degree in Adult Education and Applied Psychology from the University of Toronto.

A feminist therapist, she practices individual, couple and family therapy with St. George Counselling and Consulting Associates in Toronto.

She has three adult children—Christopher, John and Mary—two daughters-in-law, Kathleen and Jennifer, and she delights in her three small grandchildren, Ryan, Kyle and Emma. Her family now includes her husband, Lindsey Wellner, and his two grown sons, John and David.

Retreating to her wilderness lakeside cottage is a special joy. There she continues to write and enjoy the solitude.

Boynton and Dell

The authors co-lead daughter mother workshops and seminars from which came the material for this book. Both women received their Marriage and Family training at Interfaith Pastoral Counselling Centre. Both are Clinical Members and Approved Supervisors in the American Association for Marriage and Family Therapy.

Index

L

Letter Writing and Journaling 143, 147. *See also* Nine Major Options
Lisa's Story 52. *See also* Never the Twain Shall Meet
List Making 143, 146. *See also* Nine Major Options
Living From Our Core 143, 156–158. *See also* Nine Major Options
Loss xx–xxi 63. *See also* Feelings
Lower Self 156. *See* Core Energetics

M

Marcia's genogram 23-25. *See also* Genograms
Marcia's Story 26–29, 64–65, 68
Marilyn's Story xix
Mary's Story xviii
Mask 156. *See also* Core Energetics
Meditating 118. *See also* Herlooms
Mixed feelings 73
Monica's Story 164, 170

N

Negative messages 77. *See also* Destroying negative messages 81
Nerissa's Story 105–106, 130–131
Never the Twain Shall Meet 51. *See also* Relationship Styles
Nine Major Options 143
    Family Celebrations and Crises 143, 151-152
    Letter Writing &Journaling 143, 147
    List Making 143, 146
    Living From Our Core 143, 156-158
    Preparing for the First Visit Home 143, 154-155
    Researching Family Systems 143, 146
    Resolving Inner Conflicts 143, 152-153
    Self Discovery 143-144
    Visualizing What You Want 143, 151
Nothing in Common 55. *See also* Relationship Styles
    Cynthia's Story 55-56

P

Part of healing 81. *See also* Negative messages
Persephone xiii

Personal transformation 132
Positive Behaviour 97. *See also* Empowering messages
Positive Objects 97
Preparing for the First Visit Home 143, 154–155. *See also* Nine Major Options

R

Relationship Styles 47-60
    Best Buddies 49
    Friends 53-55
    Never the Twain Shall Meet 51
    Nothing in Common 55
    Strangers 57
Repressed feelings 63. *See also* Feelings
Research Jitters 44
Researching 118. *See also* Herlooms
Researching Family Systems 143, 146. *See* Nine Major Options
Resolving Inner Conflicts 143, 152–153. *See also* Nine Major Options

S

Sarah's Story 93–96, 102, 124–126, 153-154
Saying goodbye 163
Self Discovery 143–144. *See also* Nine Major Options
Serena's Story 99
Sharing 118. *See also* Herlooms
Strangers 57. *See also* Relationship Styles
    Darlene's Story 58
Sue and Peggy 179
Sue's Story 165–167
Susie's Story 103–104

T

Taking Photos 118. *See also* Herlooms
Tears xx
The Thread Goes On 189
Three Stages 64. *See also* Feelings
    Acknowledgement 64
    Expression 64
    Integration 64, 67
Triangles 18–19
    Ellen's Family Triangles 18
Triangulation 19

Other New Harbinger Self-Help Titles